EXPLORING YOUR PERSONALITY

Discovering Who You Are Through Your Sun
And Moon Signs And The Enneagram

Miriam Slozberg

BALBOA.
PRESS

A DIVISION OF HAY HOUSE

Balboa Press books may be ordered through booksellers or by contacting:

Balboa Press
A Division of Hay House
1663 Liberty Drive
Bloomington, IN 47403
www.balboapress.com
1 (877) 407-4847

Print information available on the last page.

ISBN: 978-1-9822-3362-4 (sc)
ISBN: 978-1-9822-3363-1 (e)

Library of Congress Control Number: 2019912530

Balboa Press rev. date: 09/19/2019

Contents

Introduction

I'VE HAD A challenging life, and most people have but for their own unique reasons. I always felt like the outcast, the black sheep, you name it. I was the one who was picked on during my middle-school years especially, and I had a strong dislike as well of the popular ones. Yet, at the same time, I had longed to be like them because they seemed to have had an easy life where things just came to them. That was my perception anyway and even after those days were over, I felt the same, and still feel that way.

And the truth is, I am the outcast, the eccentric one, the black sheep, you name it! But that is not such a bad thing, is it? Back in the day, I did think it was a bad thing, and I was made to believe it was a bad thing. Over time, I realized that it is better to be the oddball than to be a clone. Clones are boring and don't think for themselves, and well, the oddballs are unique and are quite fascinating, to say the least. The latter is better which is something I learned as I had gotten older due to just being worn down from all of the bullshit that life has thrown at me. It is better to be creative, intuitive, and the type to march to your own drum. This is one of the reasons why I had developed a strong interest in astrology.

In fact, astrology has been a strong interest of mine for the longest time, and I was certified as an astrologer as well back in 2006 through the Astrology Career Institute. For a while, I had veered towards past life astrology which is something that I still practice on occasion. I got away from it for a while due to my struggles with personal issues that I will not bring up here which was causing my depression to get out of control. But things are better and well-managed now and this is why I am back at it.

However, I practice astrology a little different these days. This is what urged me to write this book! I now incorporate parts of the Enneagram model in my readings, and I will be sharing how that works in this book. The first thing I will do is give you a very brief intro on the history of astrology, as well as the Enneagram model. And I am not an expert of the Enneagram, so the work I have added in this book are from the following: GI Gurdjieff, Oscar Ichazo, Dr. Claudio Naranjo, Katherine Chernick Fauvre and David W. Fauvre, MA for 27 Enneagram Tritypes, Don Riso and Russ Hudson.

In fact, because the Enneagram has been an interest of mine for a while which meant I have been studying it, does not make me an expert. I am an astrologer, not an Enneagram coach or teacher. I learned a lot more about the Enneagram while working directly with Katherine Chernick Fauvre who had been a big help for me writing this book.

However, let's save the Enneagram for a bit later as we will focus on astrology for the moment.

Brief History Of Astrology

ALRIGHT, THE HISTORY of anything can be somewhat boring and I will spice it up and keep it brief. I will only say that the points that I will bring up in this book are derived from one of the best references around, which is *The Only Astrology Book You'll Ever Need* that was written by the late astrologer and author, Joanna Martine Woolfolk, in 2012. However, for now, you may not know what astrology really is or even know the difference between astronomy and astrology.

Astronomy is the scientific study of the planets, and astrology is a pseudo-science that involves interpreting the effects of the planets on our lives. Astrology just does not only apply to people, but it applies to animals, events, natural disasters, you name it, astrology has an effect on it.

Astrology dates back to ancient times when civilians of Mesopotamia started to observe the planets in the sky. And, the Babylonians in 1900 BC, approximately discovered that the planets had some type of effect on human life and they had also discovered the zodiac. That is when they found that the planets were moving through those constellations and found that the movement of the planets moving through those constellations were affecting their day to day lives. They began to tie major events which included disasters to these transits.

Astrology then evolved ever since as the Greeks had their own take on it, the Indians did as well, and finally, astrology was used in western cultures many centuries later.

The only problem is that once astrology had made it into the western culture, the practice was not taken very seriously by many. This is how those so-called horoscopes in newspapers had made the practice appear to be something not to be taken seriously due to its laughable predictions.

The fact of the matter is, with that said, the horoscopes you read in newspapers and on websites are never accurate because these so-called predictions are only based on the sun sign. The sun sign only makes up a fraction of who you are, even though it is an important fraction, it is still just a fraction.

Anyone's personal horoscope is made up of their Moon sign, their Rising sign or Ascendant which was the sign rising at the time of their birth, as well as the other planets, the houses they are placed, and the transits that were happening at the time of their birth. That is a lot more complex than the sun sign alone which is why horoscopes that you read in the newspaper cannot be taken seriously.

There will be more about the planets, the signs, and the houses covered later on in the book. In the next part of this introduction (and the last), the Enneagram model will be covered.

Brief History Of The Enneagram Model

YOU MAY HAVE heard about the Enneagram but you don't know what it really entails. The Enneagram or the 'Enneagram of Personality' is a model which represents the psyche and represents the 9 personality types. The word Enneagram comes from the Greek words, *"ennea"* which means nine and *"gramma"* which means something that is written or even drawn. The ancient symbol has its roots in antiquity.

The Enneagram symbol was introduced to the West by GI Gurdjieff, a Russian mystic, philosopher, spiritual teacher, and composer originally of Armenian and Greek descent. He was extremely passionate about spiritual pursuits and traveled to Central Asia, Egypt, Iran, India, Tibet, and Rome and then returned to Russia. He began teaching his philosophy, The Fourth Way, using the Enneagram Symbol to his first students in 1912. He later traveled to Western Europe and then North America. He was always unforthcoming about the source of his teachings.

The "Enneagram of Personality" was created by a Bolivian mystic, Oscar Ichazo. Ichazo introduced the 'Enneagram of Personality' 10 month intensive to a group of his spiritual seekers in 1968 just outside of Arica, Chile.

One of his Ichazo's students was a Chilean spiritual seeker and psychiatrist, Dr. Claudio Naranjo. From 19971-1973 Naranjo taught study groups called 'Seekers After Truth" in Berkeley, California.

The purpose of the Enneagram is to show people how their personality types are affecting them, and how they can make the best use of their personality types. This model has shown people how to become more self-aware and has given them an opportunity to show them how they can be the best people that they can possibly become. The Enneagram is a great tool to use for self-development.

And, when you tie the Enneagram model with astrology, then you really gain even more insight about yourself which will be even more beneficial. You will not only become more self-aware, but you will figure out the path that you really are meant to take! This will eliminate any confusion that is standing in the way when it comes to the path you need to take whether this has to do with career, your relationships, and anything else that would be highly important to you.

Now, before we start talking about the Enneagram, let's put that aside from now and delve back into the basics of astrology. You will see later on how both tie with one another perfectly.

Astrology 101

HOW YOU KNOW about the basic history of astrology, and in this section, you will be learning about the roles the sun, moon, and rising sign play in your life. You will also learn about the other planets, the zodiac signs, as well as the houses which all make up your personal horoscope.

And once you learn about that, you will then realize why those daily or weekly horoscopes that you read in the newspapers or on websites are total bullshit. However, in order to start, let's just compare your personal horoscope to an onion.

You have to peel one layer after another to get to the nitty-gritty of your personal horoscope, the same way as you would with an onion. However, I am going to cut to the chase and not go into irrelevant detail about what each planet means other than the sun, the moon, and the rising sign, as well as the houses. With that said, I will start with the cliff notes version of each planet, as well as the zodiac signs so that everything is covered. Then I will focus more on the important stuff. Let's start right now!

The Planets And
Their Meanings

THE REASON THAT anytime anyone asks you what your sign is, you will automatically tell people your sun sign because that is all you know about based on your birth. And, with that said, even though the sun sign is a fraction of your horoscope, it is a highly important one. The other planets are important as well, but the sun is the most prominent planet in your personal horoscope.

- **The Sun** - This planet represents you as a whole. It represents your key motivations, your vitality, your likes, your dislikes, and your ego. The Sun also indicates your identity and how you express yourself.
- **The Moon** - This planet represents your instincts, your emotional attachments, your emotional response to stimuli, your conscious mind, and your habits. The way you express your emotions is governed by your Moon sign.
- **Mercury** - This planet represents how you communicate, how you learn, how you solve problems, the things you are curious about, as well as where your general interests lie.
- **Venus** - This planet represents your social skills, the way you interact with others, the type of partners you are attracted to, and how you attract your partners as well. This planet also indicates what you consider as beautiful, as well as your spending habits. This is also the planet of luck.
- **Mars** - This planet represents your motivation, your inner drive, confidence, where you put your energy, aggression, the way you express anger, your sex drive, as well as how you take initiative. When you go after something you really need or want, that is the influence of Mars behind your actions to get there.

- **Jupiter** - This planet represents growth, your ethical nature, the areas of abundance, and knowledge. This is the planet of luck. However, even though Jupiter is lucky, it can also be the cause of over-indulgence as well.
- **Saturn** - This planet is frowned upon because it represents restrictions, limitations, lessons in life, and even where you don't feel adequate. But this planet is a no-nonsense planet which means if it is well used, it also represents your practical side, caution, safety, boundaries, as well as hard work. Saturn means business.
- **Uranus** - Have you stopped laughing at the name yet? If not, once you do, then read further because it has nothing to do with what you are laughing about. This planet represents your unconventional side, the areas of freedom you want to seek, and your rebellious side. It also represents intuition, the unexpected, sudden changes, and innovation.
- **Neptune** - This planet rules creativity, illusion, imagination, and also where you can be easily deceived.
- **Pluto** - This is a powerful planet that represents where your power lies as well as transformation.
- **Chiron** - This is the planet that represents the areas of your life where you are wounded and as a result, you can pass on the wisdom that you have learned from it. This is why Chiron is the wounded healer.

Alright, now you know about the role of the planets, Let's now pick apart the zodiac signs and what they represent.

The Zodiac Signs
And The Houses

NOW YOU KNOW about what the planets mean, and you are now ready to learn about what each of the zodiac signs represents. Each sign represents an element, and a planet or planets rule each sign, and some planets are exalted in each sign which means they do quite well and feel at home there. And, some planets are in their detriment in their signs which means they are weak, and the planets that are in fall in each sign means that they are quite unwelcome and don't do well. Let's now begin examining each of the 12 signs.

- **Aries** - This is the first sign of the zodiac and it is a fire and cardinal sign. Mars rules Aries, the Sun is exalted, Venus is in its detriment, and Saturn is fall. This is the sign that represents boldness, independence, leadership, passion, drive. However, the downside of Aries is that the sign can be pushy, impatient, aggressive, and self-centered. The saying for Aries is *I am*, and the Ram is the icon.
- **Taurus** - This is the second sign of the zodiac and it is an earth and fixed sign. Venus rules Taurus, the Moon is exalted, and Pluto and Mars are in its detriment, and Uranus is fall. This sign represents stability, security, tenacity, patience, loyalty, love, and need for material which includes food. However, the downside to Taurus is stubbornness, materialism, possessiveness, resistance to change, and indulgence. The saying for Taurus is *I have*, and the Bull is the icon.
- **Gemini** - This is the third sign of the zodiac and it is an air sign, and it is mutable. Mercury rules Gemini. This sign represents communication, versatility, activity, variety, connectivity, intelligence, adaptivity, and information. The downside to Gemini, however, is deception, exaggeration,

cunning traits, and lack of structure, and consistency. The saying for Gemini is *I think*, and the twins are the icon.

- **Cancer** - This is the fourth sign of the zodiac and it is a water sign, and it is cardinal. The Moon rules Cancer, and Jupiter is exalted, and Saturn is in its detriment, and Mars is fall. The sign represents emotion, a love for family and home, nurture, compassion, support, healing, and unconditional love. However, the downside of Cancer is dependency, possessiveness, moodiness, and emotions that are out of control. The saying for Cancer is *I feel*, and the crab is the icon.
- **Leo** - This is the fifth sign of the zodiac and it is a fire sign, and it is fixed. Sun rules Leo, and Neptune is exalted, and Uranus and Saturn are in its detriment. This sign represents warmth, playfulness, charisma, generosity, bravery, protection, and fun. However, the downside to Leo is that it can be egotistical, domineering, stubborn, controlling, and vanity. The saying for Leo is *I will*, and the lion is the icon.
- **Virgo** - This is the sixth sign of the zodiac, and it is an earth sign, and it is mutable. Mercury rules and is exalted in Virgo, and Pluto and Venus are fall. This sign represents modesty, organization, order, logic, altruism, humility, and responsibility. However, the downside of Virgo is the critical nature, obsession, perfectionism, and paying attention to too many unimportant details. The saying for Virgo is *I analyze*, and the virgin is the icon.
- **Libra** - This is the seventh sign of the zodiac, and it is an air sign, and it is a cardinal sign. Venus rules Libra, and Saturn is exalted, the Sun is in its detriment, and Pluto is fall. This sign represents charm, diplomacy, harmony, beauty, balance, and fairness. However, the downside to Libra is that it can be superficial, hypocritical, indecisive, and passive-aggression. The saying for Libra is *I balance*, and the scales are the icon.
- **Scorpio** - This is the eighth sign of the zodiac and it is a water sign, and it is fixed. Pluto and Mars rule Scorpio, Uranus is exalted, and Venus is in its detriment, and the Moon is fall. This sign represents passion, protection, drive, determination, perception, and sacrifice. However, the

downside to Scorpio is possessiveness, jealousy, clinginess, revenge, paranoia, and destructiveness. The saying for Scorpio is *I desire* and the scorpion is the icon.

- **Sagittarius** - This is the ninth sign of the zodiac and it is a fire sign, and it is mutable. Jupiter rules Sagittarius, and Mercury is in its detriment. This sign represents ambition, luck, optimism, enthusiasm, versatility, morality, and exploration. The downside however to Sagittarius is gluttony, restlessness, laziness, tactlessness, blind optimism, and irresponsibility. The saying for Sagittarius is *I see*, and the centaur is the icon.

- **Capricorn** - This is the tenth sign of the zodiac and it is an earth sign, and a cardinal sign. Saturn rules Capricorn, Mars is exalted, and the Moon is in its detriment, and Jupiter is fall. The sign represents drive, passion, determination, strategy, discipline, persistence, and responsibility. However, the downside to Capricorn is greed, pessimism, fear, ruthlessness, rigidity, and misery. The saying for Capricorn is *I use*, and the goat is the icon.

- **Aquarius** - This is the eleventh sign of the zodiac and it is an air sign, and it is fixed. Uranus and Saturn both rule Aquarius, and Mercury is exalted, the Sun is in its detriment, and Neptune is fall. The traits of the sign are innovation, intelligence, humanitarianism, friendliness, and altruism. However, the downside to Aquarius is detachment, being scattered, being impersonal, and being irresponsible. The saying for Aquarius is *I know*, and the water bearer is the icon.

- **Pisces** - This is the twelfth sign of the zodiac and it is a water sign, and mutable. Jupiter and Neptune rule Pisces and Venus is exalted, Mercury is in its detriment and fall. The traits of the sign are intuitiveness, mysticism, compassion, sensitivity, and an appreciation for the arts. However, the downside of Pisces is escapism, dependency, self-pity, not being realistic, and being submissive. The saying for Pisces is *I believe*, and the fishes are the icon.

That sums up the summary of the signs. Now, let's take a quick peek at the houses in your horoscope which represent the areas of your life:

- **First House** - This is the house that is naturally associated with Aries, and it rules who you are in general, it is the house of yourself which means anything from your appearance, your likes, dislikes, and general preferences. This house starts off with the rising sign or your Ascendant which is the mask you have, as well as how you view life in general.
- **Second House** - This is the house that is naturally associated with Taurus, and it rules your material values, security, and talents.
- **Third House** - This is the house that is naturally associated with Gemini, and this house indicates your style learning and communication, short-distance travel, as well as your relationships with your siblings and neighbors.
- **Fourth House** - This is the house that is naturally associated with Cancer, and this house indicates your home and family life in general, as well as the more nurturing parent. It can also represent your old age as well.
- **Fifth House** - This is the house that is naturally associated with Leo, and it indicates your leisure activities, your creativity, romance, recreation, and children.
- **Sixth House** - This is the house that is naturally associated with Virgo, and it indicates your work ethic, the type of work you are involved with and its environment, your health and your health habits, pets, and general duties.
- **Seventh House** - This is the house that is naturally associated with Libra, and it indicates your relationships, partnerships, as well as marriage.
- **Eighth House** - This is the house that is naturally associated with Scorpio, and it is a complex house that indicates your life secrets, sex, psychology, your needs, as well as joint resources. This is the house that is also associated with death.
- **Ninth House** - This is the house that is naturally associated with Sagittarius and it indicates your faith, exploration, higher education, long-distance travel, and association with different cultures.

- **Tenth House** - This is the house that is naturally associated with Capricorn and it indicates your general reputation, your career, your ambitions, prestige, as well as your authoritative parent.
- **Eleventh House** - This is the house that is naturally associated with Aquarius and it indicates your friendships, causes, associations, and wishes.
- **Twelfth House** - This is the house that is naturally associated with Pisces and it is a complex house just like the Eighth, but even more complex. This is the house that represents your deep secrets, your phobias, your subconscious, psychological issues, and your past lives. This means if you have a phobia that has an unknown trigger, it could very well be from a past life, and that can be found in this house.

Now that sums up the houses or the areas of your chart. And just because these houses are naturally ruled by the corresponding signs, that does not mean that is the case for just everyone. The sign that represents each house is determined by the rising sign. For instance, if your rising sign happens to be in Libra, then that means your personal horoscope is flipped. This means the seventh house in your case would be ruled by Aries.

Now that you know what you need to know about the planets, the zodiac, and the houses, it is time to start getting more into the nitty-gritty as the next chapter will go over the Sun, Moon, and rising signs, and their meanings.

The Meanings Of The Sun, Moon, And Rising Sign

I N THIS CHAPTER, I will go over what the Sun, Moon, and Rising sign mean in your horoscope. I will make it short and sweet and get right to the point. You may already be aware of these characteristics that I am about to present to you, but I have to throw it in here anyway.

Let's start off with what the meaning of your sun sign, and you will also display the sun sign characteristics as well based on the house where your sun is located.

Aries Sun or Sun in the First House

If you were born between the dates of March 21 to April 19, your sun is in Aries, and this is what gives you those bold, confident, initiative, and adventurous traits. You focus a lot on yourself, however, you also tend to be impatient, self-centered, and impulsive. You aren't the only one in the world that matters, Aries.

Taurus Sun or Sun in the Second House

If you were born between the dates of April 20 to May 20, then your sun is in Taurus. You have a strong appreciation for your belongings, talents, your routine, and your security. This also makes you quite loyal. However, you can be stubborn to a fault because you don't like change, and you do not like spontaneity. You will only make changes if you are ready and that can take a lot of time for you to come to terms with. You also may get carried away with eating or shopping too much, which you will regret later on but perhaps not enough to stop.

Gemini Sun or Sun in the Third House

If you were born between the dates of May 21 to June 20, then your sun is in Gemini. You are quite communicative, you are great with multitasking, you embrace change, you like to learn, and you need to be kept busy. However, at the same time, you lack consistency and you can play a game of Dr. Jekyll and Mr. Hyde. Enough is enough Gemini.

Cancer Sun or Sun in the Fourth House

If you were born between the dates of June 21 to July 22, then your sun is in Cancer. You are the mother of the zodiac because you love to nurture, protect, and you value home and family. You are quite compassionate and empathetic. However, you can be overly emotional and moody to a fault. Settle down Cancer.

Leo Sun or Sun in the Fifth House

If you were born between the dates of July 23 to August 22, then your sun is in Leo. You are highly creative, playful, and childlike. You are also assertive and vibrant, however, let's face facts. Leo is the King or Queen of the zodiac so that means you can be dramatic, possessive, egotistical, and have the need to be the center of attention. And yes, I can say those things because I know this for a fact since my sun is in Leo.

Virgo Sun or Sun in the Sixth House

If you were born between the dates of August 23 to September 22, then your sun is in Virgo. You are quite dependable, analytical, patient, health-conscious and have a good work ethic. However, you can also be quite judgemental, obsessive, and critical. Stop it, Virgo. Nothing is perfect and accept that.

Libra Sun or Sun in the Seventh House

If you were born between the dates of September 23 to October 22, then your sun is in Libra. You are charming, love to be social, need balance, want justice, you have an appreciation for beauty, and you can be quite loving. However, you can be cunning due to not wanting to deal with confrontations, which means Libras can lie most definitely. You can also be lazy and indecisive. You need to learn to fend for yourself and make up your mind, Libra.

Scorpio Sun or Sun in the Eighth House

If you were born between the dates of October 23 to November 21, then your sun is in Scorpio. You are passionate, charismatic, protective, complex, and are highly intuitive because you are a great problem solver. However, you can be very secretive, manipulative, and downright nasty. I can relate to some of this since this is where my house is at. You will never want to piss off a Scorpio but you will want to earn their trust and become a friend because you will be fiercely protected.

Sagittarius Sun or Sun in the Ninth House

If you were born between the dates of November 22 to December 21, then your sun is in Sagittarius. You are optimistic, adventurous, gregarious, have a love for learning, and quite sociable. But you can be irresponsible, restless, and blunt. Sometimes you have to face the fact that you have to be serious and responsible, Sagittarius. Life is not all about fun and games and perhaps you can learn that from your Capricorn friends.

Capricorn Sun or Sun in the Tenth House

If you were born between the dates of December 22 to January 19, then your sun is in Capricorn. You are highly organized, responsible, serious. and willful. However, you are also demanding, rigid, and you don't think fun is necessary. Capricorn, lighten up and learn something from the sign before you. You need to have a healthy balance of fun and business.

Aquarius Sun or Sun in the Eleventh House

If you were born between the dates of January 20 to February 18, then your sun is in Aquarius. You are inventive, innovative, unconventional, intelligent, humanitarian, friendly, but you can be quite distant and non-committal. Sometimes Aquarius, you need to play by the rules no matter how much you hate it.

Pisces Sun or Sun in the Twelfth House

If you were born between the dates of February 19 to March 20, then your sun is in Pisces. You are creative, intuitive, psychic imaginative, empathetic, and romantic. However, you also can be illusional and wistful, and you need to learn to ground yourself, Pisces.

Now you know a little bit of why your sun sign's characteristics may not be 100 percent fitting. That is because the house where your sun is located has a great influence on you more than you think. In some cases, even more so than the zodiac sign. If you are an Aries but you seem to be more like a Gemini and had discovered that your Sun is in the third house, then you just had your ah-ha moment.

However, this is only a piece of what you are about. Let's now go over the Moon signs and find out you are affected by your own.

Your Moon Sign

YOUR MOON SIGN represents how you respond to emotional stimuli, and it represents your instincts. The house where your Moon is at also has an influence as well. Your Moon sign is the sign the Moon was in while you were born. Let's quickly go over the Moon signs and their characteristics right now.

Aries Moon or Moon in the First House

Those who have this Moon sign or placement are quite fiery and hot-tempered, and if they have a will, they always find a way. Their desires feel like needs and that is why they go after them very hard. They love the excitement and don't like to sit still. They have to be on the go often.

Taurus Moon or Moon in the Second House

Those who have this Moon sign or placement love cozy places, luxurious environments, and they love food. They also have plenty of possessions that they don't really need but it provides them the security they think they need. They hate change and are creatures of habit. I get it since my Moon is in Taurus.

Gemini Moon or Moon in the Third House

Those who have this Moon sign or placement have a need to keep learning, and they always find ways to express themselves. They also enjoy socializing and need stimulation so they don't become bored. Boredom is quite bad for the Gemini Moon.

Cancer Moon or Moon in the Fourth House

Those who have this Moon sign or placement are constantly going through emotional changes based on their environments. If they are in a calm setting, then they are calm but if the setting they are in makes them uneasy, then that is how they become as well. My Moon is in the fourth house so to some degree I can relate.

Leo Moon or Moon in the Fifth House

Those who have this Moon sign or placement are highly creative and need to find outlets to express their creativity. They may enjoy doing artwork or writing to do that. They are also quite warm and have a knack for kids.

Virgo Moon or Moon in the Sixth House

Those who have this Moon sign or placement need to be in an organized setting or else it will be quite upsetting to them. They also have a tendency to overanalyze things but they also look for ways to be helpful to others as well since this is a service-oriented sign.

Libra Moon or Moon in the Seventh House

Those who have this Moon sign or placement are most content when they are in a peaceful situation and are naturally the type to mediate others when a disagreement is happening. They don't like to be alone and do their best when they are in relationships.

Scorpio Moon or Moon in the Eighth House

Those who have this Moon sign or placement are extremely private and will only give out information if they feel there is a need. They will not give out information easily otherwise due to their need for privacy. They look for experiences that will change them, and they are looking to have deep connections but they also make their boundaries clear.

Sagittarius Moon or Moon in the Ninth House

Those who have this Moon sign or placement have a need to travel, to learn, and are constantly having the need to explore the unknown. They also have a deep appreciation for foreign cultures, and those who have learned to speak different languages for the sake of it, then chances are they have a Sagittarius Moon or have a ninth house placement.

Capricorn Moon or Moon in the Tenth House

Those who have this Moon sign or placement have a need to achieve and be successful with what is important to them. They will be quite focused when it comes to going after what they want, and they take their responsibilities and accomplishments seriously. They have to be reminded often that they need to take a break in order to recharge so they are able to be productive and have a greater chance of being successful with what they do.

Aquarius Moon or Moon in the Eleventh House

Those who have this Moon sign or placement will not be overly emotional in the traditional sense, but they make what they value clear. This means they can be easily fueled when they have a need to advocate for a cause. They also have a desire to do the right thing, which means they will easily make sacrifices to do so.

Pisces Moon or Moon in the Twelfth House

Those who have this Moon sign or placement are extremely empathetic and are psychic. They are highly creative and generous as well and can become too emotional quite easily, and have a hard time containing their emotions. Those who have this Moon sign or placement need to embrace their creativity by taking advantage of creative outlets.

Those are what you need to know about the Moon signs or placements. And finally, let's go briefly over the rising sign or Ascendant.

Your Rising Sign

YOU HAVE ALREADY learned about the planets, the houses, and the zodiac signs. Now, you are about to learn about the importance of the rising sign or your Ascendant.

The rising sign is the sign that was rising at the time of your birth which determines your first house cusp, and this is the sign that indicates your overall disposition, your mannerisms, and it can even have an effect on your appearance, but not always. Let's go over how the rising sign has an impact on you:

Aries

Those who have this rising sign are quick, direct, and can be quite competitive. They tend to blow up easily even over insignificant issues. However, they rarely hold grudges and are quite independent. The way those who have this rising sign walk is swift, and they can be quite physically strong.

Taurus

For those who have their Ascendant in Taurus are seen to be laid back, easy-going, and they are quite tenacious and can endure a lot. However, they have explosive tempers if they are pushed. Those with this rising sign tend to overindulge in eating, drinking, and shopping. They are solid and can easily become overweight as a result.

Gemini

Those with this rising sign are quite alert, quick, and are quite communicative. There is a charm about those who have the Gemini Ascendant and they are quite sociable. Those who have the Gemini rising sign are also unable to sit still and don't like to be in one place for too long. They are highly energetic and can be slender as a result.

Cancer

The individual who has their rising sign as Cancer tends to be the homebody type, and don't deal with rejection too well as they become too sensitive easily. This individual is seen as shy, subdued, and also possessive. Those with this rising sign tend to overeat as well as they like to indulge a sweet tooth too often. Often times, as a result, they are overweight.

Leo

Those with Leo rising sign are quite strong, magnetic, optimistic, and are usually quite popular. They can be quite generous, but also at the same time loud and want to be the center of attention. Their mannerisms are quite exaggerated.

Virgo

People with the virgo rising sign are quite critical of themselves and of others and can be too hard on themselves. However, they are usually quite modest, tactful, honest as they don't want to beat around the bush, and conservative. They are worry-warts, and likely have uneven nails due to frequent nail-biting.

Libra

Those with this rising sign are quite sensitive and don't function well when there is chaos in their surroundings, as they want to maintain balance. They are also quite sociable and know how to make friends easily, and they also have a love for the high life and have luxurious tastes as well. They tend to move gracefully as well.

Scorpio

Those with this rising sign are powerful, intense, and quite secretive. They also have a hard time trusting others as they are naturally suspicious, and will be prone to digging into the backgrounds of those who they don't trust. They, in fact, know how to uncover people's secrets. They are also usually quite successful in achieving their goals because they don't let anyone get in the way of them. They also tend to have piercing eyes because of how intense they are.

Sagittarius

Those who have this rising sign like to be around people, yet at the same time, need their independence and freedom. They can be quite witty, blunt, cheerful, but their moods can change easily due to their environment. They are usually adaptable and have a need to be in different places as they don't like to sit still. Their mannerisms tend to be exaggerated like the Leo rising folks.

Capricorn

These individuals with this Ascendant are quite serious and melancholic. Those with this rising sign are quite ambitious and are determined to succeed in whatever is important to them. They can be seen as snobs based on the fact that they only want to associate with those who are wealthy or who rank high status wise. They seem to be snobbish, unapproachable, and cold.

Aquarius

Those with this rising sign seem to be detached and even aloof, however, at the same time, they are smart, kind and have a strong interest in humanity. They are also quite genuine, and want to socialize but only on a superficial level, unlike the Libra who wants relationships. They tend to wear clothing that appears to be eccentric and stand out, and they would be the ones who would love having inked bodies.

Pisces

Those with the Pisces rising sign are very easy-going, and at the same time, can be emotional. However, they get along with almost everyone, and they are not known to be aggressive at all. They want to look for the best in everyone and in every situation which gets them hurt because they are idealistic when it comes to that and don't face the reality that many people do not possess good qualities and that many situations are downright shitty. They are eager to help when they can because they are naturally kind.

That concludes Astrology 101. You are wondering why I am stopping there since there is more to astrology such as planetary transits, progressions, and retrogrades. Yes, that is true, this is only a fraction of astrology. The fact is that those other parts to astrology that you hear about are not relevant to this book. This is about finding your true personality based on your core astrological elements in conjunction with the Enneagram model, which will be covered in the next chapter. We are still a bit of a way off from getting to the goods but you need to learn about the basics of astrology, which you just did - and now you will be learning about the basics of the Enneagram model in the next chapter, Enneagram 101.

Enneagram 101

YOU HAVE ALREADY learned about the Enneagram model in the introduction but I will repeat what it is here since astrology is being put on the back burner for now, and the Enneagram will be the focus. The Enneagram or the Enneagram of Personality is a model that represents the psyche and represents the 9 personality types.

The Enneagram model by iStockphoto

People have been interested in learning more about this model, and about their personality type so they can make improvements in their lives by connecting with the right type of people, and sticking to the most suitable type of work if they can. Even if they are happy with the status quo, they simply want to learn about this phenomenon to learn more about themselves.

In this chapter, you will learn about the 9 personality types, as well as the wings. Prepare to be blown away with what you are going to learn because now we are getting closer to the nitty-gritty. Let's start off with the personality types, which will be covered in the next section. All of the work on the Enneagram in this book is referenced through the sourced created by Oscar Ichazo, Katherine Chernick Fauvre, David W. Fauvre, and Dr. Claudio Naranjo.

The 9 Personalities

THE 9 PERSONALITIES are indicated on the Enneagram model, and once you read the descriptions of these personalities, you will most definitely get your ah-ha moment. **With the permission of Katherine Chernick Fauvre, her descriptions of each personality type are used in italics.** Let's go over them now.

Type One - The Perfectionist - The idealized image of this personality type is all about order, perfection, and needing everything done just the right way. Their core fear is a lack of perfection. However, they are known to be hardworking, disciplined, honest, and responsible. Because their core fear is lack of perfection, they can be critical of themselves and others. The planet that is associated with this type is Mercury, and the sign would be Virgo.

Their idealized image of themselves matches these sayings: *I am good, I am right, I am in control, I am responsible, I am diligent, I am appropriate.*

Their core fears match these sayings: *The fear of being wrong, bad, evil, corruptible, inappropriate, careless, irresponsible.*

Type Two - The Helper - The idealized image of this personality type is to be needed and wanted. Their core fear is not being helpful. The planet that is associated with this type is the Moon, and the sign would be Cancer.

The type Two's idealized image match these sayings: *I am caring, I am nurturing, I am helpful, I am altruistic, I am appealing, I am welcoming.*

These are their core fears: *The fear of being worthless, needy, inconsequential, immutable, unappreciated, dispensable, unhelpful.*

Type Three - The Performer - The idealized image of this personality type is being a high achiever. Their core fear is being insufficient and failing. The planet that is associated with this type is the Sun, and the sign would be Leo.

The sayings that match the type Three's idealized image are: *I am successful, I am efficient, I am competent, I am focused, I am productive, I am the best.*

Their core fears are: *The fear of failure, being inefficient, incapable, useless, unmasked, exposed, unable to do.*

Type Four - The Individualist - This idealized image of this personality type is being unique and being valued for their uniqueness. Many of them are quite artistic, as many are writers, musicians, or artists. Their core fear is being seen as inadequate and abandoned. The planet that is associated with this personality type is Neptune, and the sign would be Pisces.

The sayings that match the idealized version of the type Four are: *I am unique, I am special, I am aesthetic, I am tasteful, I am deep, I accomplished.*

Their core fears are: *The fear of being inadequate, emotionally cut off, plain, commonplace, flawed, defective, abandoned.*

I am a type Four so I can relate to all of this.

Type Five - The Investigator - The idealized image of this type is being knowledgeable, educated, wise, and having their privacy respected. Their core fears are being intrusive and not being educated enough. The planet that is associated with this type is Uranus, and the sign would be Aquarius.

The sayings that match the idealized image of the type Five are: *I am perceptive, I am knowledgeable, I am observant, I am different, I am logical, I am wise.*

Their core fears are: *The fear of intrusion, engulfed, overwhelmed, obligation, not existing, annihilation, ignorance.*

Type Six - The Loyalist - The idealized image of this personality type is being loyal and dutiful, and being safe and secure. They are secure with predictable patterns. Their core fear is being betrayed, misled, alone, and not safe.

The planet that is associated with this personality type is Saturn, and the sign is Capricorn.

These sayings match the idealized image of the type Six: *I am dedicated, I am dutiful, I am provocative, I am loyal, I am compliant, and/or I am rebellious.*

Their core fears are: *The fear of being blamed, unsafe, left alone, fear itself, tendency to submit, helpless, misled.*

Type Seven - The Enthusiast - The idealized image of this personality type is experiencing happiness, being optimistic, and being a lot of fun. Their core fears are being trapped and having limitations placed on them. They have a strong desire for freedom and the planet that is associated with this type is Jupiter, and the signs that are associated with it as well are Sagittarius and Pisces.

The sayings that match the idealized image of the type Seven are: *I am happy, I am optimistic, I am fun, I am enthusiastic, I am interesting, I am playful.*

Their core fears are: *The fear of emotional pain, missing out, being inferior, incomplete, trapped, limited, bored.*

Type Eight - The Challenger - The idealized image of this type is being powerful, bold, and being in control. Their core fear is being powerless, weak, and being vulnerable. The planets that are associated with this type are Mars and Pluto, and the sign that is associated is Scorpio.

The sayings that match the idealized image of type Eight are: *I am invincible, I am powerful, I am protective, I am authentic, I am direct, I am bold.*

Their core fears are: *The fear of being weak, powerless, harmed, controlled, manipulated, humiliated, underestimated.*

Type Nine - The Peacemaker - The idealized image of this personality type is being kind and easy-going. However, their core fear includes a lack of harmony and conflict. The planet that is associated with this personality type is Venus, and the signs that are associated are Libra and Taurus.

The idealized sayings that match the idealized image of the type Nine are: *I am kind, I am agreeable, I am easy going, I am peaceful, I am humble, I am unassuming.*

Their core fears are: *The fear of being loveless, shut out, discordant, inharmonious, complication, conflict.*

The type 9 wants peace and they are the types that want to spread kindness and positivity because everyone benefits. However, they do not want to deal with conflict and become fearful whenever there is a disruption. Sometimes they end up being walked on and many times they say yes to those who ask them for favors when they really deep down don't want to do it or can't.

You now may be wondering if all Libras are Nines, or are all Scorpios Eights. The answer to that is no, absolutely not. Just like how those who have the same sun sign can be different due to other factors in their charts. And those are just the core personalities that were covered.

These personalities can be altered when they lean towards the personalities next to them in the model. Those are called the wings, and that will be further discussed in the next and last section of this chapter.

The Wings And Arrows

YOU HAVE ALREADY read about the 9 core personality types on the Enneagram. However, that is seldom the case. That is why those who are of any personality type lean on their neighboring personality types on the Enneagram model, which are called the wings which have been talked about and shared by many sources that had originated from Dr. Claudio Naranjo.

The wings are what balances any type, and it also gives it flavor, or spice, whichever you want to call it. Here is a better way to envision how the wings influence personality. You have a plain baked potato. It is pretty boring on its own. So that means you will want to add some butter, and perhaps even some sour cream. That jazzes it up which is exactly how the wings jazz up the personality types.

People identify with one wing internally and one externally. The one they really identify with is the external one which makes them unaware of their internal one.

For instance, for someone who is a Type Three, he or she will end up falling onto their neighboring wings either Two or Four in order to alter their personalities somewhat. And they can fall on either the Two wings for periods of their lives and on the Four wings in other periods of their lives, depending on the situations they face. And some people can fall heavily onto one wing. Wings don't change the personality type, but as I said already, they add spice to it, they influence it, and it is healthy because it helps people become somewhat more well-rounded. However, it is not always expressed in a positive way. That will be explained in a bit once I start getting into the nitty-gritty of how the wings influence the personality types. Let's start going over that now!

- **Type One - The Perfectionist** - This type will only be able to lean on the Nine and Two wings. When the One leans on the Nine wing, this helps them relax somewhat. They also handle disagreements in a more peaceful way and are less judgemental as well. When the One leans more on the Two wing, they are sociable and are warmer towards others. The One can appear to be quite cold when in defense, but the Two will add warmth to them.

- **Type Two - The Helper** - This type will only be able to lean on the One and Three wings. When they lean on their One wing, they can become more laser-focused on a task that they are dedicated to finishing. They also have a much easier time saying 'no' which is something that the Twos by themselves have a hard time doing. The One wing helps them worry less about upsetting others when they look after their own needs by saying 'no'. When the Twos lean on the Three wing, they are quite comfortable with making their goals known and are also comfortable with going after them as well. They still want to be liked, but they also want to be admired.

- **Type Three - The Performer** - This type will only be able to lean on the Two and Four wings. When they lean on their Two wing, they are a lot more generous and helpful towards others and are more sensitive towards the feelings of others as well. Many professional coaches are Threes who fall heavily on their Two wings because they want to help others succeed in their professional lives. When the Threes lean on their Four wings, they may be inclined to express themselves through a form of art, and are also retrospective, and don't ignore their own feelings. They also tend to have deep conversations with others.

- **Type Four - The Individualist** - This type will only be able to lean on the Three and Five wings. Fours love to be noticed express themselves in a way that makes them unique and wants to be acknowledged and appreciated for it. However, they have a painful sense of lack that makes them feel self-conscious and it is even more so when they are not noticed. But, when they learn on their Three wing, they are more confident, energetic, and goal-oriented. They want to be visible for their achievements. When the Fours lean on their Five wings, they are more receptive, reserved, analytical, and less emotional. If a Four is having to do some research, they will put their emotions aside and lean on their Five wing.

- **Type Five - The Investigator** - This type will only be able to lean on the Four and Six wings. Fives are reserved and don't like to show emotion, but when they lean on their Four wing, they do show an emotional side to themselves and are a lot more sensitive. They also tend to fall heavily more into the arts but will stay more behind the scenes. Many Fives that lean heavily on their Four wings tend to become screenplay writers or photographers. When the Fives lean on the Six wings, they become more intuitive, loyal, and prefer to work in teams rather than working solo.

- **Type Six - The Loyalist** - This type will only be able to lean on the Five and Seven sings. Sixes are quite dependent as it is and are quite anxious and cynical. However, when they lean on their Five wings, they are able to be less reactive and are able to be calmer, and can look at things more objectively, and develop an appreciation for learning new things. Their Five wings actually help them neutralize their anxious thoughts. When the Sixes lean on their Seven wings, they become more optimistic and cheerful, but since they are still Sixes, they are cautiously optimistic if they see there is a reason to be. That is the best way to be for anyone.

- **Type Seven - The Enthusiast** - This type will only lean on the Six and Eight wings. Sevens are quite scattered, only want to have fun, and have large visions. However, when they lean on their Six wings, they are able to become more realistic about certain situations by seeing potential problems that may occur which provides them with an opportunity to problem-solve. They still see the glass half full, but they also know that it won't stay that way if a solution isn't created. When the Sevens lean on their Eight wings, they are more grounded and assertive, and find a way to put their ideas into some form of action and then go after it.

- **Type Eight - The Challenger** - This type will only lean on the Seven and Nine wings. Eights are all about wanting to be in control, and will not allow anyone or anything to get into the way of that. The Eights are naturally serious but when they fall onto their Seven wings, they actually are looking to try new things for pleasure. They are willing to let go of some control and explore their adventurous side as well. When they lean onto their Nine wings, they are calmer, warmer, and not as reactive, and will want to put their power into helping a greater cause.

- **Type Nine - The Peacemaker** - This type will only lean on the Eight and One wings. Nines are all about wanting peace and harmony and avoid confrontation at all costs. However, when they lean onto their Eight wings, they are far more assertive, grounded, and will take charge, even if they are challenged. When they lean onto their One wings, they will pay more attention to details and will be precise with their work or anything else they need to do and are more punctual as well.

After learning about wings and how they can influence the personality type, you can see how those who lean on either of their wings will become more well-rounded.

Arrows

You have just learned about the wings, and now let's focus on the arrows or the lines which they are also referred to. If you look at the Enneagram model, you will see that each point makes a connection to two other points as well, and that is quite relevant for you to know.

The arrows show you that you can take on positive and negative qualities of the other personality types that the points are connected to. That means when they are feeling secure and positive, they display the positive qualities of the numbers that are connected to their number in this particular order:

142857 1

That means if the type 1 is in a good frame of mind, then he or she will take on the positive qualities of the type 7 and 4 as well. And if the type 7 is in a good frame of mind, then he or she will take on the good qualities of the 5 and 8, and so on.

The other group that takes on the qualities of one another due to their connections are:

3 - 6 - 9 - 3

That means the type 3 will take on the positive qualities of the 6 and 9, the type 6 will take on the positive qualities of the type 3 and 9 and the 9 will take on the positive qualities of the 3 and 6.

For example, if a type 1 is satisfied that he or she attained a goal, then he or she would display the confidence the same way a type 1, 4 and 7 would. If a type 9 made a decision to go after a goal and decided to take on the appropriate action to achieve it, then he or she would display the positive traits of a 3, 6 and 9. All you need to do is read up on the strengths of each personality type in order to see the connection.

For instance, if a type 2 feels as if he or she was not appreciated by being helpful, then he or she will display the possessive and controlling aspects of the type 2. Or if a type 3 feels that he or she is failing and will not achieve what he or she was after, then the type 3 would display the anxiety and pessimism that a type 3 in stress would.

Now let's briefly look at the positive and negative traits that each type can take on based on situations that cause a positive or negative reaction.

- **Type One** - When the type one takes on the positive qualities of the 7 they become more self-accepting, optimistic, plan their activities for enjoyment, and become more spontaneous. When they take on the negative qualities of 7, they can self-destruct with substance abuse or in other ways. And when the type 1 takes on the positive traits of the 4, they become more empathetic and creative. When they take on the negative traits of the type 4, they become depressed, feel unloved, long for what they don't have, and they lose hope.
- **Type Two** -When this type takes on the positive qualities of the 4, they accept their feelings no matter how unpleasant, and express themselves in a creative way. They also express what they need a lot more, and find acceptance in being

alone. When they take on the negative side of 4, they compare themselves to others and are filled with envy. They also become quite depressed and self-absorbed. They also withdraw. When the type 2 takes on the positive qualities of 8, they are more honest, they don't beat around the bush, they are not so worried about what others think of them, and they are more confident. When they take on the negative qualities of 8, they become controlling, play the blame game, become irritable, and harden up.

- **Type Three** - When this type takes on the positive qualities of 6, they become more family-oriented, they care about what is best for a group, they acknowledge their feelings and vulnerability. When they take on the negative aspects of 6 they fear rejection, they become anxiety-ridden, indecisive, and dependent. When the 3 takes on the positive qualities of 9, they can relax, slow down, see the bigger picture, and be more at peace. When they take on the negative side of 9, they become apathetic, become passive-aggressive, numb themselves with substances, and procrastinate.

- **Type Four** - When the 4 takes on the positive qualities of the 1, they become more organized, disciplined, become great problem-solvers, and aren't controlled by their feelings. When they take on the negative side of 1, they can become judgmental, critical, and have a holier than thou attitude. When they take on the positive qualities of 2 they are there for others and connect with others as well. However, when they take on the negative traits of 2, they become dependent, ignore their needs, find ways to get attention, and can be manipulative.

- **Type Five** - When the 5 takes on the positive qualities of the 8, they get in touch with their personal power, they become more outspoken, they trust their instincts, and they can defend themselves. When they move towards 7 and take the positive quality of the type, they become fun and optimistic. When they move towards the negative side to 7, they become irresponsible. When they move towards the negative side of 8, they become unreasonable, ignore the feelings of others, and become punitive.

- **Type Six** - When the 6 takes on the positive side of 3, they become proud of their accomplishments, and take action and are more decisive. When they take on the negative qualities of 3, they can become workaholics so they can avoid the unpleasant feelings they have, they take on an image or a role for superficial reasons, and will be dishonest just to get ahead. When the 6 takes on the positive traits of 9, they see things from a broader perspective, they are more empathetic, and are able to trust more. When they take on the negative side of 9, they become apathetic, and they abuse substances to numb their feelings.

- **Type Seven** - When the 7 takes on the positive side of 5, they become more introspective, accept the good and bad about life, and acknowledge their fears. When they take on the negative side of 5, they become very self-absorbed and find ways to escape responsibilities more. They also force others to believe what they do. When the 7 takes on the positive side of 1 they become more productive and are more interested in the welfare of others instead of themselves, they also will be more objective about their options. When they take on the negative side of 1, they become very judgemental, nitpicky, cynical, and will only have an all or nothing attitude.

- **Type Eight** - When the 8 takes on the positive qualities of 2, they reveal their vulnerabilities to others and will open up more. They become gentle, loving, and show concern for others. When they take on the negative side of 2, they overreact, become dependent, they become even more demanding. When they take on the positive side of 5, they think before they act and they become more objective. When they take on the negative side of 5, they become depressed, defeated, don't take action, become paranoid, and become withdrawn.

- **Type Nine** - When the 9 takes on the positive traits of 3, they become more action-oriented, focused, energetic, and are more in control of themselves. When they take on the negative side of 3, they take on more work than they can handle, try too hard to impress others and try to earn respect for the wrong reasons. When they take on the positive traits of 6, they become more practical, direct, realistic, and outspoken.

When they take on the negative traits of 6, they become even more inactive, more rigid, and become more anxiety-ridden and are filled with worry.

Now you have a good understanding of how the Enneagram model works, and understand how each personality type can influence the others that they are connected to with the arrows or the wings.

And what does this mean to you? And how is this relevant to astrology? You are about to learn something new. Because the Enneagram and astrology combined will give you a more accurate picture of your overall personality which will give you a better picture of how you can use your gifts effectively, and how you can work around your challenges. You can use both to just become the best version of who you really are meant to be.

In the next chapter begins the examination of the sun, moon combinations mixed with the rising signs which will determine the personality type, as well as the favored wing, if there is one. And, the next chapter will start off with examining the Aries Sun combinations with the moon and ascendant which will determine the personality type and possible favored wings on the Enneagram model.

With that said, you will realize that all people who have a lot of Aries characteristics are not necessarily going to be Eights, which also goes for those who have a lot of Scorpio traits as well.

Aries Sun And Moon Combinations And Personality Types

ALRIGHT, WE ARE now heading into the nitty-gritty of things and the first sun sign that will be examined will be Aries, and the Aries sign will be looked at combined with the Moon signs, and how the rising sign can temper those combinations. I am not going to go on and on and bore you. I will be getting right to the point so you won't have to read a novel about each sun and moon combination. Let's now get started!

Aries Sun and Aries Moon

Those who have this combination are going to be the ultimate go-getters but with more of an impatient and explosive side to them. They have a strong independent streak and will not allow anyone to influence them in any way. They will do their own thing when they want and don't care for what others think and say. They will not stand for anyone getting into their way, and this is even more prominent if they have a lot of fire or a heavy Scorpio influence and/or a 1st or an 8th house, or a 10th house stellium (the most planets in a house) in their charts, or if their Ascendants are in Aries, Taurus, Virgo, Scorpio, Capricorn, or Aquarius. Those who have these particular placements will be a Type 8 on the Enneagram model.

The Aries Sun and Aries Moon combos that have Gemini, Leo, Sagittarius in their charts, or have a stellium in their 5th, 7th, 9th or 11th houses will lean more towards a Type 7, whether they have a type 8 personality and a heavy 7 wing or are a type 7 that lean onto to a type 8. Those who have Cancer or Pisces rising signs in their charts, or a stellium in their 12th house or in houses 2, 3, 4, or 6 may either be a type 8 that leans heavily on their 9 wing. Or, they may more likely end up not being a type 8 at all and maybe a type 1 that does not rely on either of their wings. They will keep to themselves but will be expecting perfection from themselves and from others.

Aries Sun and Taurus Moon

With this Sun and Moon combination, you have the forcefulness of Aries, with the softer and tenacious influence of Taurus. This combination can make you a great leader and allow you to be more tactful with your behavior. In fact, you can focus heavily on your drive and dedication with this placement. If the rising signs are in Aries, Taurus, Gemini, Leo, Virgo, Scorpio, Sagittarius, or Capricorn, or have a stellium in their 1st, 7th, 9th, 10th, or 11th houses, then they will likely be a type 3 on the Enneagram model.

For those who have this Sun and Moon combination that have their rising sign in Cancer, Libra, or Pisces, or have a stellium in their 4th house, they may either be a type 2 or be a type 3 that leans toward a type 2. If they have the Aquarius rising sign, they may lean towards their 4 wing.

Aries Sun and Gemini Moon

Those that have this Sun and Moon combination will be having the need to talk before they think and will have a tendency to act on impulse. Those with this combination has a tendency to constantly look ahead without looking at the big picture, and will have lofty wishes. However, if they have earth in their charts as well, or if they have the Taurus, Cancer, Virgo or Capricorn rising sign which keeps them grounded, then they will be a type 3 and can lean on either wing. The house placements are not as important in this case.

However, if they have a lot of fire or have the Aries, Gemini, Leo, Libra, Sagittarius, or Pisces rising sign, then they will be a type 7. They will only want to have a good time, will be incredibly idealistic without being grounded. If they have the Scorpio or Aquarius rising sign, they may be either a type 8 leaning more on the 7 wing or a type 7 leaning on the 8 wing.

Aries Sun with Cancer Moon

Those that have this Sun and Moon combination will both have the fiery nature of Aries mixed with the watery and empathetic side of Cancer. This type is the type that will want to help others, but there is a self-centered side as the expectation to give back is there as well. This is why those who have this Sun and Moon combination with any of the fire, earth, and water rising signs will be a type 2 personality. They will be the type to help out and to give, but they will also be the type to expect you to give back. And, they will not take it well if they are not compensated for their generosity.

Those who have their rising sign in Gemini, Libra, or Aquarius will still be the type 2, but will likely fall towards the 3 wing as they will be more sociable and make more connections through networking. They are a little more detached and less possessive in this way as well but they still have a deep desire to be respected.

Aries Sun with a Leo Moon

Those that have this Sun and Moon combination are driven but warm and charming, and quite magnetic. The drive for success is also quite high, and those who have this combination tend to fall into the type 3 personality of the Enneagram model. Especially if their rising sign is in Aries, Taurus, Gemini, Leo, Virgo, Libra, Scorpio, Capricorn, or Aquarius, or that have a stellium in their 1st, 7th, 10th, or 11th houses.

Those who have their rising sign in Cancer or in some cases, Pisces may be type 3 but fall heavily towards their 2 wing, but if they have their rising sign in Sagittarius, and maybe even Pisces and/or have a stellium in their 5th, 9th, or 12th houses, then they may be a type 7. They will have lofty ideas but won't have a realistic action plan on how to attain it and can easily fall into escapist behaviors such as binge eating, drinking, or gambling if they are disappointed about not getting what they had wished for.

Aries Sun with Virgo Moon

Those that have this Sun and Moon sign combination are fired up when it comes to getting things done the perfect way. They have to get things done the right way or else they will not rest. In fact, those with this sun and moon combination can be highly critical of themselves and of others. In fact, there is a high chance that those who have this combination regardless of their rising sign and house placements will be a type 1. The only difference is if their rising signs are Cancer, Leo, Libra, or Pisces, they may fall towards their 2 wing heavily. If their rising sign is in Gemini, Sagittarius, or Aquarius, then they may fall towards the 9 wing.

Aries Sun with Libra Moon

Those who have this Sun and Moon combination are charming, idealistic, witty, and sociable. Those with this placement tend to have a more peaceful demeanor as the Libra Moon significantly softens up the Arian traits, which is why those who have this sun and moon combination are quite easy-going and they also tend to not want to face conflicts. With that said, those who have this placement will likely be the Type 9. However, the wing that is favored will depend on the house placements as well as the rising signs.

Those that are Gemini, Leo, Libra, Sagittarius, and Pisces rising sign and/or have a stellium in their 3rd, 4th, 5th, 7th, 9th, 11th, and 12th houses may be a core 9 type and will only lean on either the 8 or 1 wing when a situation arises that makes then inclined to do so. However, if they have the Aries, Scorpio, Capricorn, or Aquarius rising sign, and/or have a stellium in their 1st, 8th, or 10th houses, then they will lean heavily on the 8 wing. If they have Taurus, Virgo, or Aquarius rising sign, and/or if they have a stellium in their 2nd or 6th houses, then they may lean more towards the 1 wing, or may even be a Type 1 that leans heavily on the 9 wing.

Aries Sun with Scorpio Moon

Those who have this Sun and Moon combination are incredibly intense, powerful, strong-willed, and have a need to be in control except for when they are feeling overly stressed, then they have a need to retreat. However, those who have this placement will be a type 8, and will be a core 8 as well if their rising sign is in Aries, Virgo, Scorpio, or Capricorn, and/or have a stellium in the 1st, 2nd, 6th, 8th, and 10th houses.

However, if have their rising sign in Gemini, Leo or Sagittarius, and/or a stellium in their 3rd, 5th, 7th, 9th, or 11th houses, then they will still be a type 8 but will lean more towards a 7 wing to enjoy having some fun and to lighten up. If their rising sign is in Taurus, Cancer, Libra, Aquarius, or Pisces, and/or if they have a stellium in their 4th or 12th houses, then they will lean towards a 9 wing and they are the most likely to be the type to retreat in the face of conflict due to being overly stressed.

Aries Sun with Sagittarius Moon

Those who have this Sun and Moon combination are incredibly outspoken and have lofty ideas, and are extreme risk-takers. They are rarely grounded, do not have realistic ideas, and easily act on impulse and go for excitement. This is why those that have this sun and moon combination are going to fall into the type 7 personality. However, their rising sign can modify that somewhat.

In fact, those who have the Aries, Taurus, Virgo, Scorpio, or Capricorn rising sign and/or has a 1st, 8th, or 10th house stellium will likely be more of a type 8, even so, more a type 7 leaning on their 8 wing which also depends on what else in their personal horoscope could be influencing them. Those that have the Taurus rising sign or a full 2nd house may be a type 7 leaning heavily on an 8 wing. However, if they have the Gemini, Leo, Sagittarius, or Pisces rising sign, or have a full 3rd, 5th, 7th, 9th, or 11th house, then they will be more of a core 7 leaning on whichever wing they need to when the time is suitable.

Those that have the Cancer, Libra, or Aquarius rising sign, and/or has a full 4th or 12th house may lean more towards the 6 wing to keep them more grounded, cooperative, sensitive, and cautious.

Aries Sun with Capricorn Moon

Those who have this Sun and Moon combination are extremely dynamic, have an intense drive to succeed, and will not allow those to get the upper hand that easily. Control is what you would be all about with this combination which is why those who have their sun in Aries and moon in Capricorn would be a type 8 without a doubt. However, depending on their rising sign and house placements will cause them to favor one wing over another.

Those who have the Aries, Taurus, Virgo, Scorpio, Capricorn, or Aquarius rising sign and/or if they have a full 1st, 2nd, 3rd, 6th, 8th, or 10th house will likely be a core 8 and will only lean on the wings if a situation influences them to do so. If they have Gemini, Leo, or Sagittarius rising sign, and/or if they have a full 5th, 9th, or 11th house, then they will lean on the 7 wing more often which will lighten them up. If they are Cancer, Libra, or Pisces rising sign and/or have a full 4th, 7th, or 12th house, then they will lean heavily onto the 9 wing which will also make them have a peaceful demeanor.

Aries Sun with Aquarius Moon

Those who have this Sun and Moon combination have some interesting qualities as they are quite likable, sociable, and have a knack for seeing the uniqueness in everyone who you meet, but there is no tolerance for bullshit and this is the type that marches to their own drummer. Some who have this sun and moon combination have the drive to succeed with their own unique goals which may be different from the norm which depends on the other placements in their personal horoscopes as well.

Those who have this sun and moon combination will either be a type 3 that leans heavily on their 4 wing, or a type 4 that leans heavily on their 3 wing. Those who have their rising sign in Gemini, Cancer, Leo, Libra, Sagittarius, or Aquarius, and/or that have a full 3rd, 5th, 7th, 9th, or 11th houses are going to be more charming, sociable, as well as driven but are willing to cooperate with others will be a type 3 but will still lean heavily on the 4 wing because of embracing their unique nature. Some may be type 4 but will rely heavily on their 3 wing which will depend on how else their personal horoscope influences them.

Those who have the Aries, Taurus, Virgo, Scorpio, or Pisces rising sign, or have a full 1st, 2nd, 4th, 6th, 8th, 10th, or 12th house will be less cooperative and will have a more eccentric approach to themselves. They will also be the type to express their uniqueness in ways that others may find to be obnoxious which will put them in the type 4 category which will cause them to lean on the wings that is the most fitting for them depending on the situation.

Aries Sun with Pisces Moon

Those who have this Sun and Moon combination will have their Arian traits buried quite deep as the watery Moon takes over. They are more introverted, soul-searching, and self-analytical and are not overly confident but have a strong independent streak at the same time. This type is quite introverted and those who have this sun and moon combination will fall into the type 5 regardless of their rising sign and house placements.

Those who have this placement will fall into the 5 personality type and depending on the situations that fall into their lives, they may lean toward the 4 or 6 wings. Those who have communicative signs such as the Gemini, Sagittarius, or Aquarius rising sign may lean towards the 4 wing which causes them to be more expressive, however. But overall those that have this sun and moon combination are going to be the type 5.

If your sun is in Aries, and you know your Moon and rising sign, you will know what your personality type is on the Enneagram model. The next chapter will cover the personality types of those who have their sun in Taurus.

Taurus Sun And Moon Combinations And Personality Types

IF YOU ARE a Taurus and you are curious to know what your personality type on the Enneagram model happens to be, then you are in luck because you are about to find out based on your sun and moon sign combinations! That also will depend on your rising sign and house placements as well. But for the most part, the sun and moon combination will say a lot! Let's start off now!

Taurus Sun with an Aries Moon

This sun and moon combination is powerful, as it causes those who have this to be driven and to be very goal-oriented and want to be successful. In fact, the traits are quite similar to those who have an Aries sun and Taurus moon combination. The difference is that the softness from the Taurus is more prominent than the fiery energy from Aries. However, those who have this placement are going to be a type 3 personality.

Those who have their rising sign in Aries, Taurus, Gemini, Leo, Virgo, Scorpio, Sagittarius, and Capricorn and/or who have a stellium in their 1st, 2nd, 3rd, 5th, 6th, 7th, 9th, 10th, or 11th houses will be a core type 3 and will lean on wings 2 or 4 whenever the situation arises for them to do so. However, for those that have the Cancer, Libra, or Pisces rising sign may lean towards the 2 wing. Those who have Aquarius rising, and/or have a stellium in the 4th, 8th, or 12th houses may lean more towards the 4 wing as their passions may be more on the eccentric or creative side.

Taurus Sun and a Taurus Moon

Those with this sun and moon combination are going to be quite stubborn and will be quite tenacious so they reach their goals in the best way possible. They also follow the rules and will not accept anything that is less than perfect in their eyes. Those who have this sun and moon combination are going to be a type 1 personality. And, those who have Aries, Taurus, Virgo, Scorpio, and Capricorn and/or a stellium in the 1st, 2nd, 3rd, 4th, 6th, 8th, and 10th houses will be the most rigid which means they will be the true core 1 type and will only lean on wings 9 and 2 when necessary.

For those who have their rising sign in Gemini, Cancer, Leo, Libra, Sagittarius, Aquarius, or Pisces and/or have a stellium in their 5th, 7th, 9th, 11th, or 12th houses will either lean towards a 9 type or a 2 wing.

Taurus Sun and a Gemini Moon

This is a tricky sun and moon combination. The Gemini moon mixed with a Taurus sun softens the rigidity somewhat and causes those who have this placement to be more social. However, many times opinions and judgments are formed without good reasoning, and jumping to conclusions happens a lot with this placement. There are trust issues that come up without a good reason as well. This is why those who have this placement would be a type 6 personality. However, those who have the Gemini, or Aquarius rising sign, and/or a full 3rd, 9th, or 11th houses tend to fall towards the 5 wing as they are more likely to observe and do research of their own.

Those that have Cancer, Leo, Libra, Sagittarius, or Pisces rising, and/or has a stellium in their 5th or 7th houses will lean more towards the 7 wing as that helps them lighten their points of view. The rest of the rising signs and placements would mean they would be more of a core 6 type and lean on either wings whenever any situation would arise for them to do so.

Taurus Sun and a Cancer Moon

Those with this sun and moon placement are a contradiction, as they are quite sensitive to others and are eager to please even though they are still stuck in their own ways of thinking. They are true people pleasers and do what they can to avoid conflict. They can be passive-aggressive as well if they are not happy with someone but refuse to speak up just to avoid conflict. This is why those with this placement have the 9 type personality.

However, those who have Aries, Gemini, Leo, Scorpio, Sagittarius, or Capricorn rising and/or have a full 1st or 10th house will lean towards their 8 wing heavily in order to go after what they want even if that means speaking up and experiencing conflict to deal with it. Those who have the Taurus, Virgo, or Aquarius rising sign and/or has a full 3rd or 6th house will lean heavily on their 1 wing as it will help keep them self-serving and less of a "people pleaser". They will also tend to their own needs more this way as well.

Taurus Sun with a Leo Moon

This sun and moon combination may sound like one that is tough to handle but this is a great one as it helps you go after what you want and to be successful. You are sociable and honest even to a fault, but you know how to work well with people and this is excellent for a manager or for a boss to have. Those who have this placement will be a type 3 personality. Those who have Cancer, Libra, or Pisces as their rising sign and/or a stellium in their 6th, 11th or 12th houses will fall more towards a 2 wing as this gives them a knack for helping others.

Those who have Gemini, Leo, Scorpio, or Aquarius as their rising signs and/or has a full 4th, 5th, 8th, or 9th houses will lean more towards their 4 wing as they will have more of an eccentric or an artistic, yet a highly emotional side that will cause them to stand out more.

Taurus Sun with a Virgo Moon

This earthy combination is great for those who love to learn and observe and great for having excellent common sense. However, they also never tend to get too far only because they don't like conflict and don't like to impose, and they also possess a great gift where they see everyone as having a unique way about them. This part of them can be quite beneficial for those who want to encourage others to see their unique gifts and what they can offer. Most of those who have this placement will be a type 5 that leans heavily onto a 4 wing with most placements.

However, those who have Cancer or Libra rising signs, and for those that have a stellium in their 7th houses may learn more towards a 5 personality type and 6 wing as they tend to be more social.

Taurus Sun with a Libra Moon

Those that have this sun and moon combination are known to charming, idealistic, optimistic, and there is also ambition in there as well. Those who have this placement can be quite expressive, as well as dramatic, and will want to make themselves known as well for something that they are good at. They are positive by nature and will be able to accomplish whatever their mind sets them to do so because of the strong Taurean nature. But they don't handle adversity too well. Those that have this sun and moon placement will have a type 4 personality but will rely heavily on their 3 wing.

Those who have fiery signs such as Aries, Leo, or Sagittarius, or who have a full 1st or 10th house may be a type 3 personality that leans heavily on their 4 wing as the additional fiery nature would cause them to be more of the go-getting types.

Taurus Sun with a Scorpio Moon

This placement is contradictory by far. An intense emotional side is masked by a charming exterior. However, there is a strong stubbornness with this placement as well as an all-or-nothing attitude. And with this placement, there is the determination for going after what is wanted and will not allow anything or anyone to get into their way. However at the same time, if there is a threat that a competitor will get what this individual is going after, then this person who has this placement won't be emotionally strong enough to fight for it and may allow the competitor to go after it since the need to retreat is stronger than fighting.

Those who have this placement will be a type 8 but will lean heavily towards the 9 wing due to the fact that even with the strong will, confrontation can be painful if the opponent has more to offer. Rising sign and house placement won't have such an effect on this because this placement is quite powerful as it is.

Taurus Sun with a Sagittarius Moon

Those that have this placement are quite social and charming by nature and want to go and have a good time. The adventurous side to them is obviously influenced heavily by the moon sign since the sun sign is anything but that. However, those who have this placement have very high standards and will only want to hang around those who are appealing to them. Otherwise, they would rather be alone than to hang with people who they don't consider to be interesting. Those who have this placement regardless of their rising sign or house placements will be a type 7 personality and will lean heavily on the 6 wing due to the Taurean influence.

Taurus Sun with a Capricorn Moon

This sun and moon combination gives those who have this placement a stable, practical, and down to earth personality. But they are also friendly, dependable, and will be there to help those in need. But with this combination, they will not want to waste time and they will be focused on getting any type of task done perfectly. They will not accept any of their work that is done less than perfect which is why those who have this placement will be a type 1 but will lean heavily on their 2 wing due to their helpful and dependable nature.

The house placements and the rising sign will not have much of an influence on this personality type, however, those with this placement with different rising signs may go after their wants and wishes in different ways, the determination is the same nevertheless.

Taurus Sun with an Aquarius Moon

Those who have this sun and moon combination are diplomatic, friendly but detached, studious, logical thinking, inventive, hard-working, but may struggle with inertia due to the inner fear of change as they have a strong desire for stability. Those who have this placement are known to be friendly but are rarely successful in the material sense. This is why those who have this placement are a type 6 personality but lean heavily on the 5 wing.

Those who have their rising signs in Aries, Virgo, Scorpio, Capricorn or Aquarius regardless of the house placements may fit more like a type 5 personality while leaning heavily on their 6 wing as they are the types to prefer to be alone more but still possess a friendly nature.

Taurus Sun with a Pisces Moon

This sun and moon combination will create a kind but dreamy and heavily artistic individual which also creates a private dreamy life. The sun sign is practical and grounded which is an asset to those who have this placement as even with their private dream life, they know what is real and what is not, and will stick to reality when they know they must be responsible such as managing work and family affairs. However, those who have this placement can be maladaptive daydreamers due to the fact that it is comfortable, and those who have this placement are emotionally sensitive.

Those with this placement can also be used by others who would see their kindness as their weakness. However, the good thing is that these types are intuitive and will sense those who are using them. Their Taurean stubborn streak will usually come to their rescue by not allowing themselves to be used.

With that said, those who have this sun and moon combination would be the type 4 personality. However, those who have Virgo, Scorpio, or Aquarius as their rising signs and/or have a stellium in their 4th, 6th, 8th, or 12th houses will lean heavily towards the 5 wing due to the fact that they will be less sociable and would prefer to study and observe the world around them.

This completes the Taurus Sun and Moon type and Enneagram personality combinations. The next chapter will cover the Gemini Sun and Moon combinations in addition to the rising signs if they are influential in any way to determine the personality type on the Enneagram model.

Gemini Sun And Moon Combinations And Personality Types

THE ARIES AND Taurus Sun and Moon combinations have been examined, and now in this chapter, the Gemini Sun and Moon combinations will be examined to determine what the likely personality type would correspond with those - which also depends on the rising sign and other significant factors in the horoscope. Let's start now.

Gemini Sun with an Aries Moon

Those who have this sun and moon combination are going to be ambitious, charming, smooth-talkers, and will know exactly what they want and how to get it. They are determined and quite competitive. That is why the personality type that fits this sun and moon combination would be the type 3 personality on the Enneagram model.

However, those who have Cancer, Libra, or Pisces rising, and/or who has a full 6th, 7th or 11th house may lean heavily on the 2 wing as they will be there to help others reach their goals as well. And those who have Scorpio, Aquarius, or Pisces rising, and/or have a stellium in the water houses (4th, 8th, and 12th) will tend to lean heavily on the 4 wing as they also will have a dramatic, eccentric, or artistic side to them as well.

Gemini Sun with a Taurus Moon

With this sun and moon combination, people are similar in many ways to those who have a Gemini sun and an Aries moon. However, with this placement, people who have this are more sociable and even more charming. They are happy to give a helping hand to those in need but will immediately know when someone is trying to take advantage of them. The ambitious personality is quite strong like their Aries moon counterparts. Those who have this placement regardless of the rising sign and house placement will be a type 3 personality and will lean quite heavily on the 2 wing.

Gemini Sun with a Gemini Moon

Those who have this sun and moon combination are highly electric as they are full of energy, are always looking for excitement, and need to constantly be busy. They are quite sociable, and are great talkers, but have a difficult time sticking to one task at a time. They are constantly looking for ways to learn and are looking for new experiences as well. Those who have this sun and moon combination will be a type 7. However, for those who have Taurus, Cancer, Virgo, Libra, or Aquarius as their rising signs, and/or a full 6th, 7th or 11th house will lean more towards the 6 wing which will bring them back down to earth so they can not only prefer to work in teams but this will help them become a better judge of character.

Those with this placement that have the Aries, Scorpio, or Capricorn rising sign and/or who have a full 10th house may lean more towards the 8 wing which will also bring them down to earth but will be competitive in nature and be in control of their actions.

Gemini Sun with a Cancer Moon

Those that have this sun and moon combination are going to be inquisitive but yet very emotional and will be the type to march to their own drummer. And, those with this combination will be more tense, anxious, and can easily become depressed due to thinking too much. However, this is an asset for those who want to concentrate on a particular field and will help them remain laser-focused which is great for their studies or career, or any project that they want to take up. At the same time, if they focus on their personal problems, then they can become dragged down and depressed. This is why those who have this sun and moon combination will be a type 4 personality.

However, those who have Aries, Gemini, Leo, or Libra as their rising signs and/or have a full 1st, 7th or 11th house may lean more towards the 3 wing which will help them become even more ambitious. If they have Taurus, Scorpio, Capricorn, or Aquarius as their rising signs and/or have a full 3rd house, then they will lean more towards the 5 wing which will help them become inventive and even more studious.

Gemini sun with a Leo moon

With this sun and moon combination, nothing is more happy-go-lucky than this one, well actually that is not true but it is one of the most happy-go-lucky sun and moon combinations around. This is the ultimate people person but can be quite fickle unless the mind is made up. Once the mind is made up, then this individual will be reliable.

However, if not, then there is no focus and this individual will be bouncing around from one thing to another. This is why with this sun and moon combination, those who have it will be a type 7 but more often than not will lean on the 6 wing especially when their minds are made up regardless of their rising sign and house placements.

Gemini sun with a Virgo moon

Those with this sun and moon combination will be likely to be driven by anything that will feel them any type of knowledge and anything that is intellectually stimulating. Those with this placement are nervous and can focus on insignificant worries, and frequently feel that they are misunderstood. They march to their own drummer, and will not want to be told what to do by anyone, or more importantly, they will not want to be told what to think. They have excellent ideas but do not execute them as much as they talk about them. They like to explain and share their theories to others even if there is not much substance. Those who have this placement will either be a type 4 or a type 5.

Those who have Cancer, Leo, Libra, Scorpio, Sagittarius, or Pisces rising signs, and/or have a full 3rd, 4th, 7th, 8th, 9th, 10th, or 12th houses will be more likely a type 4 leaning heavily on a 5 wing, or a type 5 leaning heavily on a 4 wing which depends on their other components in their horoscopes. Those who have Aries, Taurus, Gemini, Virgo, Capricorn, or Aquarius rising, and/or has a full 1st, 2nd, 5th, 6th, or 11th houses will be a type 5 or a type 4 that leans heavily on their 5 wing which will cause them to be more inventive and studious.

Gemini Sun with a Libra Moon

Those that have this sun and moon combination are going to be pleasure-seeking, charming, and sociable, and highly idealistic. They love trying out new adventures with their friends, but hard work does not seem to thrill them as they can be irresponsible unless they have some strong earth qualities in their charts.

With that said, those with this sun and moon combination will be a type 7. However, if they have Taurus, Virgo, Scorpio, or Capricorn rising, or if they have a full 6th or 10th house then they may lean on their 8 wing which will bring them more ambition and help them become more practical as well which means they have a better chance of achieving something by taking proper action.

Gemini Sun with a Scorpio Moon

Those with this sun and moon combination will be deep thinkers, emotional, and quite intuitive. Even with the Scorpio moon, this is not a leader combination. In fact, those with this sun and moon combination can be influenced somewhat from those who they look up to, yet at the same time, those with this combination will not hesitate to take chances if they feel there is a reason to do their own thing. They may be influenced by those who they look up to what may be a positive or negative thing, but they also are the type to march to their own drummer. Those who have this placement will be a 4 type.

For those that have the Libra, Capricorn, or Aquarius rising sign or that have a full 7th or 10th house will lean more towards the 3 wing to help them become more ambitious and become more focused, and an action taker. For those who have Taurus, Virgo, Scorpio, or Pisces as their rising sign or have a full 3rd house or a full water house (4th, 8th, or12th) then they will lean more towards the 5 wing which will cause them to be more of a researcher and learner, and more of a hermit.

Gemini Sun with a Sagittarius Moon

For those who have this sun and moon combination will be pleasure-seekers, will have a need to go on any type of adventure, and are all for fun and spontaneity. And without a doubt, those with this sun and moon combination will fall into the 7 type personality. However, if they have Taurus, Cancer, Virgo, Libra, or Aquarius, and/or if they have a full 7th or 11th house, then they will fall more towards the 6 wing as it will help them cooperate and work with others. If they have the Aries, Scorpio, or Capricorn rising sign, and/or have a full 10th house, then they will lean more towards the 8 wing which will give them a sense of control, direction, and ambition.

Gemini sun with a Capricorn moon

This sun and moon combination creates a shrewd, ambitious, go-getting, but a friendly personality which means that those who have this placement will be a type 3 personality. If they have Cancer, Virgo, Libra, or Aquarius as their rising sign or have a full 6th, 7th, or 11th house, then they will lean more towards the 2 wing which will give them a reason to help others by teaching others their skills so they can succeed.

For those who have Aries, Leo, Scorpio, or Pisces rising, or have full water houses (4th, 8th, 12th), then they will lean more towards the 4 wing which will cause them to march to their own drummer, be more emotional, and even artistic.

Gemini sun with an Aquarius moon

Those who have this sun and moon placement are going to be one of those with a quick mind, a progressive way of thinking, and with a strong sense of intuition that will allow you to think outside of the box if you see that a change is needed. You are a great communicator and have a humanitarian trait as well. You can see both sides of a given story, and you can also be quite fascinating to be around. This is why those with this placement will be a type 3 personality that heavily leans on a 4 wing regardless of the rising signs and house placements.

You are naturally going to be a go-getter by thinking outside of the box, with a fascinating and an unusual side that people will be drawn to. The only thing is if you have a full water house (4th, 8th, and 12th) you may be more withdrawn and would prefer to interact and do business online instead of being in person but your traits will not change otherwise.

Gemini sun with a Pisces moon

This particular sun and moon placement can be tricky for a person to have as they are highly sensitive and intuitive, but would be the type to observe, learn, and study from a distance and absorb information without being a true expert on anything. You tend to have a strong need to escape the world and its issues by retreating in your own world.

Without strong ambitions, you are stable and happy when you are in an environment that is peaceful as you are high strung with stress. You have a strong artistic side and you also feel that you are often misunderstood that can bring you a lot of frustration. This is why with this combination; you are a type 4 that leans heavily on the 5 wing which gives you a Bohemian type of personality.

However, if your rising sign is in Virgo or Capricorn or if you have a full 10th house, then you may possibly lean towards the 3 wing instead of the 5 as those placements will give you the drive to be ambitious and more grounded.

This is what the Gemini Sun and Moon combinations bring out, and if you have a Cancer Sun, you will want to read the next chapter as you will learn about the personality type that you most likely would be based on your sun and moon combination.

Cancer Sun And Moon Combinations And Personality Types

FOR THOSE WHO have a Sun in Cancer, it may be believed that the main personality type would be a 2 on the Enneagram model because of the nature of the sign. However, that isn't the case too often. And, you will see that as you read through the sun and moon combinations below, starting with the Aries moon.

Cancer Sun and an Aries Moon

Those that have this combination are naturally suspicious in general, cannot be fooled but have a lot of determination and self-respect, but not in a narcissistic way. Those with this combination believe in the Golden rule, *treat others as you would want to be treated*. Quick thinking and saying smartass comments is a trait as those with this combination rarely get offended by what others say. Instead, they are given a smartass response. Those who have this sun and moon combination will be a type 6 personality and will lean heavily on the 5 wing as they prefer to keep to themselves and observe the world.

However, those that have a Sagittarius rising sign and/or a full 5th or 9th house may possibly lean towards the 7 wing because even with the suspicious side, those with these traits may be more adventurous.

Cancer Sun and a Taurus Moon

Those with this sun and moon combination are charming, kind, and well-liked, and determined in their own way. However, they can be blunt and honest if they need to be, but in a gracious way. Those with this combination are going to be sincere and loyal, sometimes to a fault. That is why the personality type that matches those with this sun and moon combination is type 9, and will likely lean towards the 8 wing regardless of the rising sign and house placements. They are kind to a fault, somewhat passive in some ways but when push comes to shove, then a fight will be on, but in a tactful and mature manner.

Cancer Sun and a Gemini Moon

Those that have this sun and moon combination are intuitive, sensitive, kind to a fault, and have a tendency to withdraw, and think too much to the point of procrastinating. In fact, they may try something new but will fail to stick to it due to finding something new that is appealing. Those that have this sun and moon combination will be the 9 personality type.

However, those who have the Aries, Scorpio, or Capricorn rising sign and/or a full 10th house will lean more towards the 8 wing which will ground them and will give them a reason to fight for what is important and to speak up. Those who have Virgo rising or a full 6th house will lean more towards the 1 wing which will help them become more organized and procrastinate a lot less. And, they will be more likely to finish what they started.

Cancer Sun and a Cancer Moon

Those who have this sun and moon combination are extremely emotional, are there to help at the drop of a hat, and have this need to be needed. However, if they feel they are ignored or not appreciated, they become very upset and will let those who had snubbed them know about that. This sun and moon combination make a type 2 personality.

However, those that have the Virgo rising sign or a full 6th house will lean towards the 1 wing as they will be more altruistic and purposeful without expecting back. Those who have Aries or Capricorn rising sign or a full 10th house will lean towards the 3 wing as they will be more ambitious and slightly less emotional.

Cancer Sun with a Leo Moon

Those with this sun and moon combination will appear to be quite sociable, positive, confident and demanding at the same time of respect. Even though those with this combination have self-respect, they want to be the ultimate winners and the most successful in their social circles and will achieve that due to their determination. They can come off as self-righteous and have little patience for those who are sloppy and who don't measure up in any way. Those who have this placement are a type 3 personality.

Those that have the Cancer, Virgo, or Pisces rising sign, and/or has a full 6th house may lean towards the 2 wing and will be more selfless and help others succeed. Those who have the Cancer, Scorpio, Aquarius, or Pisces rising sign, and/or have full water houses (4th, 8th, or 12th) will lean more towards the 4 wing and be more dramatic, artistic, and eccentric.

Cancer Sun and a Virgo Moon

Those with this sun and moon combination are known to be cautious, the type to go by the book, and to follow the rules, and will not make any strong decisions until a proper judgment has been made. However, those who have this sun and moon placement can be quite judgmental of others, and themselves, and have a perfectionist way of being. This is why those who have this sun and moon combination are a 1 type personality.

However, those who have the Cancer, Libra, or Pisces rising sign and/or a full 6th will lean more towards a 9 wing or a 2 wing which will help them to be more accepting and less critical, or more helpful. Those who have any of these placements can lean towards either wing, which depends on what else is heavily influencing their personalities based on other important factors that could be in their horoscope.

Cancer Sun with a Libra Moon

Those with this sun and moon combination are contradictory as they crave company from others and want to be social but at the same time, they have trust issues and are highly suspicious of other people's motives - even if there is no reason for it to be which makes them introverted. Cancer and Libra do not mix well which is a huge factor, and those who have this sun and moon combination are a type 6 personality.

Those who have a Taurus, Virgo, or Aquarius rising and/or have a full 6th house will likely lean more towards the 5 wing which will make them more analytical and better judges of character. Those who have Gemini, Libra, or Sagittarius rising and/or has a full 7th or 11th house may lean more towards the 7 wing which will make them more sociable and allow them to let loose somewhat.

Cancer sun with a Scorpio moon

Those who have this sun and moon combination are incredibly emotional but to the extreme. In fact, even with a magnetic way about you, you can scare people by exploding due to intense emotional outbursts which happens a lot. And that is the one thing that prevents you from accomplishing what you want, your intense emotions get the best of you. You have a fierce and protective side and you will not allow anyone to harm those who are dear to you.

This is the result of having too much water in this sun and moon combination. You would have a type 8 personality but leaning heavily towards the 9 wing regardless of rising sign and other factors. You are fierce but you have a soft spot for those in need and for those who are dear to you. This is a powerful combination.

Cancer sun with Sagittarus moon

This sun and moon combination is contradictory because on one hand, you would prefer security and have a tendency to withdraw. Yet, on the other hand, you have an adventurous and sociable side that makes you cautious but at the same time, willing to get out of your comfort zone if you feel the need to. You are practical but progressive. Those that have this combination are a 6 type that heavily lean on the 7 wing. The rising sign and placements don't have a huge influence because the Sagittarius moon is quite strong.

However, those who have fire signs as rising signs will be even more outgoing and adventurous.

Cancer sun with a Capricorn moon

Those sun and moon combination is quite good to have as it makes you ambitious and the type to go after what you want, but you are also sensitive to the needs of others. You are kind and helpful as well and want to help others succeed. Prestige means a lot to you, and you can be quite competitive, but you will give a helping hand if necessary. This is why those who have this sun and moon combination are a type 3 personality but will lean heavily on the 2 wing due to their ambitious but helpful nature.

Those who have Cancer, Virgo, Libra, Aquarius, or Pisces as rising signs, and/or has a full 6th, 7th or 11th house will lean even more heavily on the 2 wing. However, those who have Aries, Leo, or Capricorn rising, and/or has a full 10th house will be more of a core 3 type.

Cancer sun with an Aquarius moon

This is a combination of a sun and moon that don't understand one another, but you are detached, aloof yet kind, and understanding, and can be critical of others but in a well-meaning way. You are constantly caught up in thoughts, but you have no time and patience for pettiness. Those who have this sun and moon combination have a 9 type personality but lean heavily on the 1 wing.

And, for those who have the Virgo rising sign, and/or a lot of earth in their charts in addition to a full 6th house, this may cause someone to be a 1 type but lean more towards a 9 wing. Perfection is what you want but you are also more willing to be more patient at the same time.

Cancer sun with a Pisces moon

This sun and moon combination makes you very friendly, peaceful, and intuitive, however, there is self-confidence lacking. At the same time, you can be defensive and self-protective if you really sense something is quite off. You can be quite suspicious and cautious as well. This is why those who have this sun and moon combination are the 9 type personality but can lean more heavily towards the 8 wing which will help them become more assertive and practical.

Especially, if you have the Aries, Virgo, Scorpio, or Capricorn rising sign, and have a full 1st or 10th house, then that will push you further towards the 8 wing which means you still want peace but you will stand for even less bullshit. Rising signs that are either Cancer, Libra, or Pisces, and/or have full water houses (4th, 8th, 12th) may cause you to be more of a core 9 but will lean on the 8 wing if absolutely necessary.

That sums up the personality types for those who have a Cancer sun for all of the moon sign combinations. In the next chapter, we'll look into the Leo sun and moon combinations to determine their personality type! And, here is a spoiler for you

- they are not all 3 types!

Leo Sun And Moon Combinations And Personality Types

NOW IT IS time to look at the sun and moon combinations of the Queen or the King of the zodiac and determine their personality type. You may already think that the Leo must be a 3, and in some cases that is true. However, in other cases, not at all. Let's check it all out now starting with the Aries Moon.

Leo Sun with an Aries Moon

Those who have this sun and moon combination are going to be determined, ambitious, and will take action to rectify any setback. There is a lot of drive with this sun and moon combination, as well as courage. You always have to be in control and can be even combative if necessary. With that said, it is common for this type to be a 3, but this sun and moon combination can be an 8 type as well.

Those who have Leo or Sagittarius can be more of a 3 type, but with Cancer, Virgo, Libra, Aquarius, or Pisces rising sign, they may lean towards the 2 wing to help others while they are working hard to achieve great things. That also includes them having a full 7th or 11th house. However, if their rising signs are in Aries, Scorpio, or Capricorn, and/or have a full 10th house, then they will be more likely an 8 type that will not stand for any type of control by other people and situations. They will be the ones to want to take the driver's seat no matter what and will be combative.

Leo Sun and a Taurus Moon

This is the sun and moon combination that I will be biased about since this is what mine happens to be. However, this combination most definitely creates a strong personality, which I was told I can be too much to handle at times. Yes, this is a good one for being practical, getting things done as they must be, but can be incredibly stubborn and not always being diplomatic. Holding your tongue can be done but when things matter so much to you, you will express how you feel sometimes not in the most tactful way. In other words, if someone deserves a big F-YOU, then they will get it! Admiration and empathy are what is expected of others as well.

This sun and moon combination can create a type 3 personality, that most definitely leans on a 4 wing, or a type 4 personality. Those that have Aries, Taurus, Gemini, Leo, Virgo, Libra, Scorpio, Sagittarius, or Capricorn rising signs and/or has a full 1st, 7th, 10th, or 11th house will be a type 3 achiever leaning towards the 4 individualistic wing. However, those who have Aquarius or Pisces rising signs and/or full water houses (4th, 8th, 12th) will be the 4 type. My rising sign is Sagittarius but my stellium is in the 8th house, and I am a type 4 personality that leans heavily on the 5 wing. In some cases, I have favored the 3 wing, however.

Leo Sun and a Gemini Moon

Those with this sun and moon combination are very active, especially mentally. They tend to act without thinking ahead at times, but can also create a plan of action and go after what they want. It depends on the other factors in the chart but those who are very action-oriented will create a detailed plan of action to go after what they want. However, in some cases, there is a lot of impulsivity over being excited about the next best thing. People are drawn to those with this sun and moon combination because they do make a great impression regardless.

With that said, in some cases, those who have this sun and moon type will be a type 3 but others will be a type 7. Those that are a type 3 will have their rising signs in Taurus, Virgo, Scorpio, or Capricorn and/or will have a full 6th or 10th house. They will create plans of action to achieve great things and go after it. Those who have Aries, Gemini, Leo, Sagittarius, Aquarius, or Pisces rising and/or a full 5th, 7th, 9th, or 11th houses will cause them to be more impulsive and looking for a good time without creating a proper plan of action.

Those with Cancer or Scorpio rising signs and/or with full water houses (4th, 8th, 12th) may be more of a 6 type because their thoughts will be so active that they will be suspicious of the actions of others. But may lean towards the 7 wing because they will be more willing to take chances due to their sun and moon combination alone.

Leo Sun and a Cancer Moon

Those with this sun and moon combination are kind, pleasant, and are trustworthy. Their dramatic sun is watered down, literally, by the reserved and nurturing moon. People will trust those with this combination because they are good listeners and will be there for others at any time. However, they also will not put up with bullshit and they also apply common sense to many situations. They will not allow others to take advantage of them, which means they won't allow anyone to mistake their kindness for weakness. Those who have this sun and moon combination will be a type 9 but may lean towards the 8 wing, and in some cases, the 1 wing.

Those who have the Aries, Leo, Scorpio, or Capricorn rising sign and/or has a full 1st or 10th house will lean more heavily on their 8 wing. They are peaceful and caring but will definitely speak up and in a blunt manner if there is a reason for it. Those who have the Taurus or Virgo rising sign and/or has a full 6th house will lean more towards the 1 wing which will keep them more organized and down to earth even more.

Leo Sun and a Leo Moon

This sun and moon combination will create the driving force for you to succeed, achieve the best and a lot of prestige, with a magnetic personality but will always find a way to beat the competition. This sun and moon combination creates the ultimate 3 type personality.

Those with Cancer or Virgo rising sign (sometimes Aquarius or Pisces), and/or has a full 6th house may lean more towards the 2 wing to help others along while they are still taking care of their own best interest. And those who have Scorpio and sometimes Aquarius or Pisces rising sign, and/or with full water houses (4th, 8th, 12th) may lean more towards the 4 wing, which can cause them to become somewhat eccentric, artistic, and even more dramatic in many ways.

Leo sun with a Virgo Moon

Those who have this sun and moon combination are quite critical, have high standards for themselves and others to meet, stubborn, opinionated, outspoken, but also have a strong need for attention and praise. Those who have this sun and moon combination will be a type 2 personality but will heavily lean on the 1 wing. They will help others but there are most definitely strings attached and have a need for perfection otherwise. Regardless of the rising sign and house placements, this will most likely be the case. The only difference is with fire signs as rising signs, they will be even more outspoken than usual.

Leo Sun with a Libra Moon

This sun and moon combination creates someone who has an idealistic view of life, but at the same time has their suspicions with the intention of others. And with that said, those who have this sun and moon combination are quite hesitant to reveal too much about themselves and to get involved with anything until they have done their research.

Those that have this combination are also aloof and quite emotional at the same time and would prefer to sit back and observe rather than to get too involved. Arts and beauty can be appealing to those with this combination. Those who have this sun and moon combination will be a type 5 but will either lean heavily towards the 4 wing, or lean heavily towards the 6 wing, depending on the other placements.

Those that have Aries, Gemini, Cancer, Leo, Scorpio, Sagittarius, Aquarius, or Pisces rising and/or has a full 1st, 4th, 8th, 10th, or 12th house will lean more heavily towards the 4 as they will be more emotional, unique, artsy, and hard to figure out. Those that have

Taurus, Virgo, Libra, or Capricorn rising and/or has a full 3rd, 5th, 7th, 9th, or 11th house will lean more towards the 6 wing. They will want to work with others, work in teams, and will be more sociable, but cautious.

Leo Sun with a Scorpio Moon

Those with this sun and moon combination are going to be highly emotionally charged to the point that they will need to have complete control over everything. And will become very upset if things don't go their way. They can become powerful leaders but they also can lose their cool which can easily get into the way of success in that regard. There is a lot of pride and confidence that comes with this placement, but once a challenge comes, then emotions can become out of control and that can be damaging to success.

Those that have this placement will have a type 8 personality, however, they will heavily lie on the 7 wing. They want power and control but don't always have a practical way to achieve what they want. Those that have Capricorn rising may be able to keep their emotions in check than the other signs which will cause those with that placement to achieve more success and to rely less heavily on the 7 wing, and be more of a core 8.

Leo Sun and a Sagittarius Moon

Those that have this sun and moon combination will have a strong passion for adventure, travel, and living in the future, and will choose to have fun over responsibility at any time. There is a cheerful and positive demeanor with those that have this sun and moon combination, and they are quite optimistic. They are quite extroverted and charming and have no patience for pettiness or triteness.

There is no doubt that those that have this sun and moon combination are a type 7. However, those that have Cancer, Libra, or Aquarius as rising signs and/or has a full 7th or 11th house will lean more towards a 6 wing as they will still have these attributes, but will be more cooperative to work with others. Those that have Taurus or Capricorn as rising signs and/or has a full 10th house will lean more towards the 8 wing that will give them more direction and will ground them more so they can achieve success.

Sun in Leo and a Moon in Capricorn

Those with this sun and moon combination are highly ambitious, quite sure of themselves, and care deeply about their reputation. and have a charming personality but will not stand for bullshit. Those with this sun and moon combination also have strong self-respect and also expect others to respect them. However, they tend to become depressed deep down due to the fact that the signs don't understand one another.

Those with this sun and moon combination are a type 3. However, those with Cancer, Virgo, or Libra and/or have full 6th, 7th, or 11th houses tend to lean more towards the 2 wing which will cause them to be more willing to help others succeed. Those with Aquarius or Pisces rising and/or full water houses (4th, 8th, 12th) will push them more towards the 4 wing which will cause them to be more emotional, eccentric, and artsy.

Sun in Leo with a Moon in Aquarius

Those with this sun and moon combination are known to be attractive personality-wise, warm, friendly, generous, extroverted, but highly idealistic and not committed. In fact, those with this sun and moon combination never get too involved with anything and will not want to make commitments as they flee from one thing to the next. In fact, they want to have a good time and will go from one thing to the next if it is appealing. Friendly but flaky is what best describes this type.

Those with this sun and moon combination are a type 7, but if they have Cancer, Virgo or Libra rising, and/or has a strong 6th, 7th, or 11th houses, then they will lean more towards the 6 wing which will allow them to be more cooperative while working in teams. If they have a Taurus, Scorpio, or Capricorn wing and/or has a full 10th house, then they will lean more towards the 8 wing which will ground them more, be in more control of things and help them have a sense of direction in life.

Leo Sun and a Pisces Moon

Those with this sun and moon combination will be kind-hearted, good listeners, unsure of what they want, and non-confrontational. In fact, those with this placement will have a hard time saying no to others even if they don't want to do something. There is no doubt that those with this sun and moon combination will be a type 9 personality.

However, those that have Aries, Taurus, Scorpio, or Capricorn rising and/or have a strong 1st or 10th house will lean towards the 8 wing which will help them be more grounded, allow them to fight for what they believe in if necessary, and achieve what they want. Those that have Virgo rising and/or has a strong 6th house will be more organized, punctual, and discerning.

That concludes the Leo sun and moon combinations with personality types. Let's now look into the Virgo sun combos and learn about those folks, and what they really are about.

Virgo Sun And Moon Combinations And Personality Types

IT IS KNOWN that Virgo is associated with the type 1 personality on the Enneagram model. And, there are some sun and moon combinations that will bring that personality type out even further. However, not all Virgos are type 1s and you will see that as this chapter progresses. Let's start with the Virgo sun and Aries Moon combination.

Virgo Sun and an Aries Moon

Those with this sun and moon combination are going to be critical, argumentative, and will have a strong need to be perfect. And they will demand perfection of others, and yet are not overly confident as they appear. Those with this sun and moon combination will express themselves in a way that is strong but not well-received by others. Those with this sun and moon placement will not stand for emotions that are gushy. It is quite safe to say that those with this sun and moon combination are a type 1.

However, if they have Gemini, Sagittarius, or Aquarius as rising signs and/or have a strong 11th house, they may lean more heavily towards the 9 wing which will help them relax and be somewhat less critical of others and themselves. If they have Cancer, Libra, or Pisces rising, and/or has a strong 7th house, they may lean more towards a 2 wing and will still be very much a type 1 but will also realize when others are in need, they'll help.

Virgo Sun and a Taurus Moon

Those that have this sun and moon combination tend to be anxious even though there is nothing to worry about. And, they are also hard-working, and will not stop working at something until the job is done. And, those with this sun and moon placement are quite sharp and get on with people quite well who they are comfortable with. They tend to be unconventional, and somewhat eccentric, but at the same time, a great problem-solver.

They are not ambitious or initiators and are very into their routine and security. Those with this sun and moon placement will be a type 6 but will lean heavily on a 5 wing. They are suspicious of others but will trust only a few people, and would prefer to observe the world than to participate.

Those that have Gemini, Cancer, Leo, Libra, or Sagittarius rising and/or has a full 7th or 11th house may be slightly more sociable and less stuck in routine (Gemini or Sagittarius only). However, this personality trait is the most likely with this sun and moon combination.

Virgo Sun and a Gemini Moon

Those with this sun and moon combination are great thinkers, highly observant and analytical, would very much prefer a book over a friend, and can give cold and unemotional responses to others even though they don't mean to be that way at all. That is how they do come off. There is a lot of nervous energy with this combination and the mind needs to be stimulated with books or other types of stimulation that will keep the mind active.

Those with this sun and moon combination are a type 5. Those who have Leo, Sagittarius, Aquarius or Pisces rising and/or a full 5th or 9th house may be more into the arts and more emotional as well, which will cause them to lean towards the 4 wing. Those with Cancer or Libra rising and have a full 7th or 11th house will lean more towards the 6 wing which will cause them to have a desire to work in teams or to have a few friends.

Sun in Virgo and a Moon in Cancer

Those that have this sun and moon combination are quite sensitive, peaceful, but deep down are practical, conservative, and analytical. This means those that have this placement are changeable on the outside and can be influenced by others, but they still prefer to go by the rules and to be practical about any situation. Intuition is strong with this sun and moon placement, as well as those who have it, can figure out any truth by 'feeling' it out. Those with this combination are also good judges of character.

Those who have this combination are pretty much always going to be a type 9 that leans heavily to a 1 wing. Peaceful on the outside but are analytical and practical at the same time. It does not matter what the rising sign, as well as house placements, are either.

Virgo Sun with a Leo Moon

Those who have this sun and moon combination are quite devoted to what is right and are devoted to duty instead of having the need to go after anything for the sake of personal gain. These individuals are assertive when it comes to believing in the right thing and doing the right thing. However, there is always that doubt when it comes to anything they have said or done so they will look back on it and analyze it to make sure it was done the right way. These individuals have a strong character and strong principals and want to be seen for that.

Those who have this sun and moon placement will either be a 9 type personality leaning on a 1 wing, or a 1 type personality leaning on a 9 wing. Those who have Gemini, Cancer, Leo, Libra, Sagittarius, or Pisces rising and/or have full 7th or 11th houses will be a type 9 leaning on a 1 wing. They are still non-confrontational but find a way to stay organized and to stay within the rules.

Those with Aries, Taurus, Virgo, Scorpio, Capricorn, or Aquarius rising and/or has a full 1st, 6th, or 10th house will be more of a 1 type that will have a perfectionist way of being but will be able to lean on the 9 wing to ease up.

Virgo Sun with a Virgo Moon

Those with this sun and moon placement are the ultimate observers that will keep their minds stimulated all the time by researching, studying, or reading useful material. They go by the rules carefully and are quite practical. Any type of relationship that this individual has will need to happen as long as there is a connection on the intellectual level. Otherwise, those with this placement will not be the one to socialize.

Those that have this sun and moon combination are a type 5. Those that have Gemini, Leo, Libra, Sagittarius, Aquarius, or Pisces and/or has a full 2nd, 5th, or full water houses (4th, 8th, 12th) may lean more towards the 4 wing as they will be more eccentric, artistic, and emotional. Those that have Cancer (and even Libra, Aquarius, or Pisces) and/or has a full 7th or 11th house may lean more on the 6 wing which will give them the urge to want to work in teams and to have relationships that don't always happen on an intellectual level.

Sun in Virgo and a Moon in Libra

This sun and moon combination makes those who have it peaceful, friendly but reserved, and has a need to develop relationships on an intellectual level. Those who have this placement are quite finicky when it comes to those who they associate with as well, and they prefer to go by the rules. That is why those that have this placement are a type 1 personality but will lean heavily on the 9 wing.

The rising sign, as well as house placements, will not have much of an impact as far as that goes. However, the only difference is that the things that are important to those with this sun and moon combination will vary based on rising sign and house placement.

Virgo Sun and a Scorpio Moon

Those that have this sun and moon combination are not the stereotypical Virgo. Those who have this combination are the type to believe in what they want to believe and march to their own drummer and are quite emotional as well. They can be rash and impulsive and have their own way of thinking and their own way of rationalizing. Those who have this sun and moon placement have the type 4 personality.

However, those who have Aries, Leo, Scorpio, Sagittarius, or Capricorn rising and/or has a full 10th house will be more ambitious and make better leaders as they will favor their 3 wing. Those that have Taurus, Gemini, or Aquarius and/or has a full 9th house or even full water houses (4th, 8th, 12th) will lean more towards a 5 wing, and prefer to live a more of a Bohemian lifestyle

Virgo Moon with a Sagittarius Sun

Those that have this sun and moon combination do not have strong Virgo traits but have very strong Sagittarius-like traits. Those with this sun and moon combination are highly idealistic, are always looking ahead, don't live in the moment, and have a strong sense of adventure. They are also quite creative, and those with this sun and moon combination are a type 7.

However, those that have Taurus, Virgo, or Capricorn, or a full 6th or 10th house will lean towards the 8 wing which will help ground them, and allow them to achieve their lofty goals if attainable. Those that have Cancer, Libra, or Aquarius rising and/or has a full 7th house will lean more towards the 6 wing which will help them be better judges of character and be more of a team player.

Virgo Sun with a Capricorn Moon

This sun and moon combination is one of the most practical ones that anyone can have. Those with this sun and moon combo have very high standards and put everyone up on a high pedestal, They are strong, determined, ambitious, and don't rely on anyone else but themselves to get things done. Many executives have this sun and moon combo which is not a surprise at all. Those with this sun and moon combo may be a type 1 or a type 8, depending on rising sign more than anything.

Those who have Taurus, Cancer, Virgo, Libra Aquarius, or Pisces rising and/or has a full water house (4th, 8th, 12th), or a full 6th house will be more of a type 1 as they have high standards but don't have the angst the same way the type 8 would. All other rising signs would point to a type 8 with this placement.

Virgo Sun and an Aquarius Moon

Those that have this sun and moon combination are quite practical, are always hungry for knowledge, and aloof. They can speak in critical ways that can come off the wrong way, and this type is empathetic and sympathetic but in their own unique way. They tend to want to stay out of the way and sit back and observe rather than participate. Those with this sun and moon combination are a type 5.

However, those that have fire signs as rising signs, and full water houses will lean more towards the 4 wing as they can be more expressive in their unique ways and creative. Those that have air signs as their rising signs as well as a full 7th or 11th house, they will lean more towards the 6 wing which will mean they are going to be more interested in having relationships and friendships.

Virgo Sun and a Pisces Moon

Those with this sun and moon combination are both practical and intuitive. They are highly analytical and profound at the same time. They are quite emotional, and based on the fact that they are practical and emotional at the same time, they tend to veer towards music, art, metaphysics, and anything unusual. Those with this placement don't want to be in the spotlight but end up finding themselves there because of their unusual ways. Those with this sun and moon combo are a type 4.

Those with fire signs as rising signs, as well as Capricorn rising and that have a full 7th, 10th, or 11th houses will lean towards the 3 wing because they are more ambitious, down to earth, and want prestige. Those that have air and water signs as rising signs, and/or has strong water houses will lean more towards the 5 wing and will live a more of a Bohemian lifestyle.

That concludes the Virgo sun and moon combinations, and the determination of the personality type on the Enneagram model. In the next chapter, the Libra sun and moon combinations will be examined, and you will learn what personality types result from those.

Libra Sun And Moon Combinations And Personality Types

WHENEVER YOU THINK of Libra, you would think of someone who is unable to make decisions and is passive and hates confrontations. Yes, that is true, and you would also think that all Libras would fit in the 9 type personality on the Enneagram model. However, just like the other sun and moon combinations, that is the furthest thing from the truth. And you will see that being the case when the first sun and moon combination will be covered, right now!

Libra Sun and an Aries Moon

With this sun and moon combination, this individual will hate being tied down, will love the idea of practical jokes, and enjoys to have a good laugh every now and then. They become depressed with routine and responsibility. It is safe to say that they are always looking to have a good time and these are not the types that will be easily ready to make commitments. It is also safe to say that this sun and moon combination brings out a type 7 personality.

However, those that have Cancer, Libra, or Aquarius as rising signs and/or has a full 6th or 7th house, they will be more cooperative and will be more likely to commit to having relationships. If they have Scorpio or Capricorn rising and/or have a full 10th house, they will lean more towards the 8 wing which will bring them more down to earth and increase their motivation to go after what they want. This means they will be more willing to be responsible to take action.

Libra Sun with a Taurus Moon

Those that have this sun and moon combination are friendly, outgoing, but at the same time, even though they appear that they don't know what they want, they do have goals. They just have a very slow time getting started with achieving them and tend to be procrastinators. They also don't like confrontations. However, they will speak up if someone is trashing something or someone who they believe in. That is why those with this sun and moon combination are a type 9 but will lean more towards the 8 wing. They don't like confrontations, and they are peaceful but will be blunt and go after what they want when things get tough.

Those who have Aries, Scorpio, or Capricorn rising and/or has a full 10th house will lean even more heavily towards the 8 wing. And in some cases, they may even be a type 8 but will lean heavily on the 9 wing if they have placements in their personal horoscopes that give them the energy to be in charge.

Libra Sun with a Gemini Moon

Those with this sun and moon combination are extremely communicative, need to be kept stimulated all the time whether it is intellectually or physically, are more social, and enjoy having a good party. They, however, do not have an interest in being tied down or responsible. However, they still value relationships for what it is worth. That is why those who have this sun and moon combination are a type 7 but heavily lean towards the 6 wing.

However, those who have Scorpio or Capricorn as rising signs and/or a full 10th house may actually swing the other way and lean towards the 8 wing which will make them charming, practical, and even intimidating in some ways. This will cause them to be more focused and committed to go after what they want.

Libra Sun and a Cancer Moon

Those with this sun and moon combination are peaceful, friendly, do what they can to avoid conflicts, and are very sensitive. There is no doubt that those that have this sun and moon combination fit into the type 9 personality. However, those that have full water houses may also be incredibly anxious and may be more of a type 6 instead, and that would even be more the case if they also had Scorpio rising in addition to that

Libra Sun and a Leo Moon

Those with this sun and moon combination will always be looking for a good time, will not be committed and go after the next best thing. Those with this sun and moon combination are also full of pride. It is safe to say that those that have this sun and moon combination are a type 7. However, for those that have Cancer or Libra as their rising signs in addition to a full 7th house, they may lean more towards a 6 wing which means they could be devoted to their relationships. However, they may be tempted to still have affairs, depending on what else can influence that in the horoscope.

Those that have Virgo, Scorpio, or Capricorn as their rising signs and/or has a full 10th house may lean more towards an 8 wing. They will be brought more down to earth, and will go after their goals and will not allow anyone to get into the way.

Libra Sun and a Virgo Moon

Those with this sun and moon placement are highly critical of themselves and of others, analytical, very independent, and even though they are reasonable during arguments they still end up doing what they choose and will not listen to anyone else's opinion. There is not a lot of empathy with this placement and will never beat around the bush either. Those with this sun and moon combination are a type 1.

However, for those that have Cancer and Libra as their rising signs and a full 6th or 7th house, they will lean more towards a 2 wing which will make them more empathetic and helpful even though they are still quite analytical and rigid. Those that have Sagittarius rising or a full 9th house may lean more towards a 9 wing which will cause them to relax somewhat and soften them up.

Libra Sun with a Libra Moon

This double dose of Libra can create someone who is in a dream world, highly romantic, and someone who needs attention, perhaps someone who is easily influenced, gullible, and is quite a people-person. Those with this sun and moon combination can also be quite artistic, and they have a mystical side to them. Those who have this sun and moon combination can be either a type 7 or a type 3, depending on several factors.

Those that are a core type 7 will have their rising signs in Aries, Taurus, Gemini, Leo, Libra, Sagittarius, Aquarius, or Pisces. They would also have a full 7th, 9th, or 11th house. However, those that have Scorpio as their rising sign may lean more towards the 8 wing which will cause them to cave into their powerful reserves and may use their charm for personal gain.

However, those who will be more of a type 3 will have Virgo or Capricorn as rising signs, as well as a full 2nd, 6th or 10th house. They will use that natural charm they have and become quite ambitious, and go after what they want which will give them that competitive edge.

Libra Sun with a Scorpio Moon

Those with this sun and moon combination are a contraction as on the surface they seem to be easy going and friendly but deep down they know how to penetrate and dig into things. They have a strong sense of justice and will do what they can to speak their mind or even correct the issue if they can. They also become extremely angry if they feel they have been mistreated. They have an idealistic way but they are also grounded when they need to be, and are progressive. Those who have this sun and moon combination will be a type 9 but will lean heavily on the 8 wing regardless of their rising sign and house placements.

Libra Sun and a Sagittarius Moon

Those that have this sun and moon combination are highly idealistic, are looking for pleasure constantly, looking for fun and adventure, and do not want to be tied down. They enjoy being with others and exploring with others as well. They will be the types to travel in groups. That means those that have this sun and moon combination will be a type 7 but will lean more towards a 6 wing especially if they have Cancer or Libra as rising signs, and/or has a full 7th or 11th house.

The other rising signs and house placements will pull them towards that 6 wing as well at times but may stay as a core 7, especially if they have Aries as their rising sign or a full 1st house.

Libra Sun with a Capricorn Moon

Those with this sun and moon combination are goal-oriented, value prestige, they want to be respected and admired, and are serious about the actions that they need to take to attain their goals. They have a great deal of self-esteem, and this is why those that have this sun and moon combination fall into the type 3 personality on the Enneagram model.

However, those that have Cancer, Libra, Aquarius, or Pisces rising (sometimes) and/or a full 7th or 11th house will lean more towards a 2 wing where they will help others along the way to succeed. Those that have Aquarius or Pisces rising (sometimes) and/or have full water houses will lean more towards the 4 wing. They will be more emotional and artistic.

Libra Sun and an Aquarius Moon

This sun and moon combination will create someone who is empathetic, very social, cares too deeply, but is afraid to become too attached to anyone or anything. They don't want to get too involved in other people's issues as they are unable to handle it, as they fear conflict. And those that have this sun and moon combination will also be a good judge of character and will stay away from those that are toxic. They value fairness and have a strong creative side as well. Those with this sun and moon combination are a type 9 personality.

Those that have Aries, Scorpio, or Capricorn rising and/or has a full 1st or 10th house may lean more towards the 8 wing which will keep them more grounded and help them use their keen intellect to advance themselves. Those that have Virgo rising and/or a full 6th house will lean more towards the 1 wing which will keep themselves organized and keep their lives as tidy as possible, and more decisive as well.

Libra Sun and a Pisces Moon

Those with this sun and moon combination are not a typical extraverted Libra. They are sensitive, and prefer to stay away, and observe. They are quite aloof and reserved, but the Libra influence will not cause them to become a hermit as they will become involved in situations that involve others if they feel there is a need for it. That is why those that have this sun and moon combination are a type 5 but will lean heavily on the 4 wing.

And, those that have Cancer or Libra, Capricorn, or fire signs as rising signs or a full 5th, 7th, 10th, or 11th house may be more of type 4 that lies heavily on the 5 wing. They will want to stand out a little more, be more expressive, and be seen and be heard.

That concludes the Libra sun and moon combinations and personality types of the Enneagram model. The next chapter will cover the Scorpio sun and moon combinations and the personality types!

Scorpio Sun And Moon Combinations And Personality Types

NOW WE ARE onto Scorpio, and that means we are going to be looking at the Scorpio sun and moon combinations to determine the personality types. And you may be wondering if any Scorpio would automatically be the dreaded type 8, and the answer, just like how it has been answered before with the previous signs is - no. Let's go and find out what these Scorpio sun and moon combinations create speaking in Enneagram terms!

Scorpio Sun and an Aries Moon

Those who have this sun and moon combination are realists, highly independent, but at the same time are impulsive, ambitious, and need to be in control. Those with this sun and moon combination will either be a type 1 or a type 8, depending on other factors.

For those that have the Taurus, Cancer, Virgo, Libra, Aquarius, or Pisces rising sign and/or has full water houses, or a full 6th, 7th, or 11th house will be a type 1 and may even lean towards either the 9 or 2 wing, depending on other factors in the chart. These individuals may be seen as perfectionists that will not stay away from their ideas but do have a sense of compassion towards those who may be seen as weaker. However, those that have Aries, Gemini, Leo, Sagittarius, or Capricorn rising and a full 1st or 10th house will be a type 8 as they will be less compassionate, be highly ambitious, and will not allow those to get into their way.

Scorpio Sun with a Taurus Moon

Those with this sun and moon combination are determined, ambitious, down-to-earth, and even though those who have this combination need to be in control, are quite rigid, they are also considerate of others and are generally more compassionate and empathetic. Those who have this sun and moon combination will be a type 8 but will lean more heavily towards a 9 wing regardless of their rising sign and house placements.

They need to be in control and will not allow anyone to get into the way but they also care for others and will even put others ahead of them if there is a situation that warrants it.

Scorpio Sun with a Gemini Moon

Those that have this sun and moon combination are witty, clever, and are excellent multi-taskers. They don't possess the typical fixed ways that a Scorpio normally would due to the fact that the Gemini Moon has a great influence. That means they also don't have the best concentration when it comes to sticking to one task as they will go from one thing to the next in a heartbeat, and they can be indecisive. They have the potential to be successful in anything they want but they need to utilize better concentration for that to happen. Those with this sun and moon combo would be a type 7 but would either lean more towards a 6 wing which will give them the desire to work with teams and cooperate with others or a wing 8.

Those that have this sun and moon combination and have the Cancer, Virgo, Libra, or Aquarius rising sign and/or has a full 6th, 7th, or 11th house will lean more towards the 6 wing. Those that have the Aries, Scorpio, or are Capricorn rising sign and/or have a full 1st or 10th house will lean heavily on the 8 wing which will ground them more, become excellent problem-solvers, and become successful with attaining their goals.

Scorpio Sun with a Cancer Moon

Those that have this sun and moon placement are going to be extremely emotional with all of that water, in addition to being intuitive. They tend to be emotionally aggressive and even possessive at times, depending on the situation. However, they are not overly assertive as they have a hard time saying 'no' when they are asked to do something that they don't really want to do. They are aloof but still want to please others. They do however have intense feelings which mean they can be jealous, suspicious, overly sensitive, and can easily allow their feelings to take over. With that said, those that have this sun and moon combination can either be a type 2, a 6, or a 9.

Those that are a type 2 will likely have the Cancer, Virgo or Libra rising sign, and/or a full 6th or 7th house. They will be the ones who will help others but will expect something back. Those that are a type 9 will have the Taurus, Gemini, Leo, Sagittarius, or Aquarius rising sign and/or will have a full 5th or 11th house. And those that have Aries or Capricorn rising sign and/or a full 1st or 10th house may be a type 9 but will lean more towards the 8 wing. And those that have Scorpio or Pisces rising and/or full water houses may be a type 6 which will cause them a lot of anxiety and will cause suspicion to take over.

Scorpio Sun and a Leo Moon

Those who have this sun and moon combination are determined, persistent, very self-confident, enthusiastic, and are competitive. That is why those with this sun and moon combination will be a type 3. They may be idealistic when it comes to relationships as they can be overly harsh with others, but that also comes from having a strong sense of pride. And the rising sign and the house placements don't influence this all that much.

It is possible however that those that have Cancer or Libra rising and/or has a full 6th or 7th house will lean more towards the 2 wing which will give them the trait of being more helpful and cooperative. And those that are Aquarius or Pisces rising and/or has full water houses can cause them to lean towards the 4 wing which will cause them to be more emotional, slightly more withdrawn on their own terms or eccentric, dramatic, and perhaps even artistic.

Scorpio Sun with a Virgo Moon

Those that have this sun and moon combination will be the type to overanalyze, pay attention to every small detail, and can be extremely critical of others or themselves but at the same time can give excellent advice to those that need it. They tend to expect very high standards of others. Those with this sun and moon combination are usually a type 1.

Those with mutable signs as rising signs may lean towards a 9 wing which will cause them to relax somewhat. And those with Cancer or Libra rising sign and/or a full 7th or 11th house may cause them to be more cooperative and empathetic as it would push them towards the 2 wing. But even so, those with this sun and moon placement only see what they want to see and have very high standards so this is why they would be more of a core 1.

Scorpio Sun and a Moon in Libra

Those that have this sun and moon combination are not only charming but they thrive on prestige and want to be the most respected, the most popular, and are highly competitive. They have extremely high standards, and there is absolutely no doubt that those that have this sun and moon combination are a type 3.

Those that have Cancer and Libra as rising signs, and sometimes with Aquarius or Pisces rising as well, in addition to them having a full 11th house, they may lean more towards the 2 wing which will give them the trait of being more caring and helpful. Or, those that have those rising signs and have full water houses may lean more towards the 4 wing which would cause them to be a little more withdrawn, creative, and even eccentric but will still want to make themselves quite known and important.

Scorpio Sun and a Scorpio Moon

Those with this sun and moon combination are both highly emotional yet are very controlling, and will know exactly how to dig up mysteries. Those with this sun and moon combo are not particularly cooperative, especially with the strong need to be in control and will have a hard time finding a partner unless he or she is completely submissive. Those that have this sun and moon combination are quite intense, and they can either be a type 8 or a type 4.

Those that have the Aries, Virgo, Scorpio or Capricorn rising sign and/or have a full 1st or 10th house will be a type 8 as they will have a strong need to be in control of others and of everything, and will have an explosive temper if they don't get their way. However, those that have the Taurus, Gemini, Cancer, Leo, Libra, Sagittarius, Aquarius, or Pisces rising sign and/or have full water houses will be more of a type 4. Yes, they will have incredibly intense emotions and will still have a need for control but are more likely to be eccentric, artistic, depressive, and will want to make their uniqueness not just known but highly important. They will make their mark in an intense way.

Scorpio Sun and a Sagittarius Moon

Those that have this sun and moon combination are expressive, philosophical, idealistic, and social-minded, and have a desire to help others and are loyal. However, they are also very aggressive and can easily lose their temper. Those that have this sun and moon combination are a type 9 however, they do heavily lean on the 8 wing due to the fact that they can be extremely blunt and can lose their temper easily. Those that have their rising signs in Virgo and Capricorn and/or have a full 6th or 10th house may be more grounded and will be able to achieve more by leaning on the positive aspects of the 8 wing more so than the others, which will help them succeed more. They will be able to keep their emotions and focus more in check as a result.

Scorpio Sun with a Capricorn Moon

Those that have this sun and moon combination are very ambitious, honest, shrewd, and are less concerned with popularity and more so with being true to themselves. They want to be in control but not in an aggressive way as their style is more professional, and have a great deal of integrity. They have a great deal of self-control and are trustworthy. Those with this sun and moon combination will be a type 8 but will be softened up quite a bit by leaning on a 9 wing.

In some cases they may be a type 3 but will lean heavily on a 2 wing if they are more concerned about being the best in their field but also want to help others achieve their goals. Especially if they have Cancer or Libra rising, and/or have a strong 5th, 7th, or 11th house.

Scorpio Sun with an Aquarius Moon

Those that have this sun and moon sign combination are quiet on the outside but are very deep within, and have some strong and fixed ideas. They tend to have high expectations of others and even of themselves at times, however, if they are disgusted or angry with someone, they will keep their opinions to themselves and stay calm and cool on the outside. They cannot stand those that are shallow or superficial, and they are very deep. They tend to stay behind the scenes and prefer to observe, analyze, and can be quite creative because their thoughts are so deep. Those that have this sun and moon combination can be a type 5 or a type 1.

Those that have earth signs as rising signs and/or a full 6th or 10th house are more of a type 1 as they are the perfectionist type and will make it clear when they are unhappy that someone or something is not meeting their high standards. However, those with other rising signs in other elements, and/or have full water houses will be a type 5 as they have a lot going on in their minds but stay back and observe.

Scorpio Sun with a Pisces Moon

Those that have this sun and moon combination are highly intuitive, artistic, highly emotional, imaginative and can be quite dramatic. Those with this sun and moon combination are a type 4. However, those that have Virgo and Capricorn as their rising signs and have a full 10th house may heavily lean towards a 3 wing as they will be ambitious and will want to be highly influential in something that they know that they have a gift for. And, they can be quite competitive as well if they were to encounter someone else with the same gift.

However, if they have Gemini or Aquarius as rising signs and/or have a full 3rd or 11th house, they may lean more towards a 5 wing where they prefer to observe and are not as emotional. They will live more of a Bohemian lifestyle in that case.

That concludes the Scorpio sun and moon combination analyses that determine the most likely personality types on the Enneagram model. In the next chapter, the Sagittarius sun and moon combinations will be examined, and the personality type will be determined through those analyses.

Sagittarius Sun And Moon Combinations And Personality Types

SAGITTARIUS. THE SIGN that represents expansiveness, optimism, and adventure. You'd think that everyone with a Sun in Sagittarius would have all of those traits and be a type 7 personality as well. Well just as you had learned that not every Scorpio is a type 8 and that every Leo is not a type 3, you will not be surprised to learn that not everyone that has a sun in Sagittarius is a type 7 personality either. Let's look into that right now.

Sun in Sagittarius and an Aries Moon

Those with this sun and moon combination are ambitious, initiating, expressive, sincere, and domineering but not in a cruel way. Those with this sun and moon combination are the ones who want to achieve great things and with that said, those with this combo are a type 3.

Those that have Cancer or Libra as rising signs and/or has a full 7th or 11th house may lean more towards a 2 wing as they would be more helpful. And those that have Aquarius or Pisces rising and/or has full water houses will learn more towards the 4 wing and be more likely into the arts and may be somewhat eccentric.

Sun in Sagittarius and a Moon in Taurus

Those that have this sun and moon combination are extremely idealistic and can be in a dream world. They are quite creative and are quite sensitive. They become hurt emotionally easily if they are insulted and will not let it brush off of them like it is believed that a typical individual with a Sagittarius sun would be. With this sun and moon combo, this would create a type 4 personality.

Those that have the Virgo or Capricorn rising sign and/or a strong 1st or 10th house may lean more towards the 3 wing which will ground them and give them a reason to be ambitious to achieve something. Those that have Aquarius rising may lean more towards the 5 wing as they would live a more of a Bohemian lifestyle and not be as sensitive.

Sun in Sagittarius and a Moon in Gemini

Those that have this sun and moon combination are always looking for the next best thing but also are ambitious and want to keep achieving prestige and have the ability to be financially successful. They are ambitious but are not always stable enough to focus on one thing. Most of the time, those with this sun and moon combination are a type 7 but heavily lean on an 8 wing. They have a sense of adventure and the need to explore that a type 7 has but are also ambitious and can be grounded if they have to be. They also have a strong way with words that will influence others.

The rising sign and house placements are not overly relevant as this sun and moon combination strongly suggests that those who have it will have this personality type.

Sagittarius Sun and a Moon in Cancer

Those that have this sun and moon combination are highly idealistic, intuitive, emotional, a visionary, and artistic. Those who have this sun and moon combination can either be a 4 or a 9. Those that have the Virgo, Scorpio, Aquarius, or Pisces rising sign, and/or has full water houses may be more of a 4 as they are more withdrawn and have an eccentric side.

Those that have the Gemini, Cancer, Libra or Sagittarius rising sign and/or a full 7th or 11th house are more of a type 9 as they are more social than the type 4s but are highly sensitive and don't want to face conflict. Those that have the Aries, Taurus, Leo or Capricorn rising sign and/or has a full 10th house may lean on an 8 wing if they are a type 9 personality or a 3 wing if they are a type 4. The rest of their chart will determine which personality type they are.

Sun in Sagittarius and a Moon in Leo

Those that have this sun and moon combination are warm-hearted but very ambitious with prestige being highly important to them. They are honest, and will help others, and have a strong sense of teamwork but will be the one to lead. Those that have this sun and moon combination will likely be a type 3 that leans heavily on the 2 wing.

The rising sign and house placements don't have too much of influence other than how heavily the 2 wing is leaned on. They are still competitive and want to be the most influential but will help others achieve their own stuff at the same time - as long as they don't feel threatened.

Sun in Sagittarius and a Moon in Virgo

Those that have this sun and moon combination are picky but not too a fault, and they have their own ways of rationalizing but at the same time are not overly critical of themselves and of others. They have a direct way of expressing anything that is important, have been known to achieve good things, can look through every small detail and analyze it, and are quite realistic with the way they view things. They are honest but well-respected.

Those with this sun and moon combination can be either a type 1 that leans heavily on a 9 wing, or a type 3 personality. Those that are a type 1 with a wing 9 would have Cancer, Libra, Virgo, Sagittarius, Aquarius or Pisces rising sign and/or has full water houses. Their standards can be quite high due to their analytical nature, but they know how to relax a lot more than the typical type 1 and this is why they lean heavily on a 9 wing. Those that have Aries, Taurus, Gemini, Leo, Scorpio or Capricorn rising and/or has a strong 1st, 7th, or 10th house may be more of a type 3 as they will want to only achieve great things and earn prestige.

Sagittarius Sun and a Libra Moon

Those that have this sun and moon combination are peaceful, friendly, tolerant, and prefer to live in a state of peace and harmony.

They don't like conflicts but if they do get into one, they will make their point clear. They are also somewhat grounded and will be able to go after a goal that they have been wanting to attain. However, for the most part this sun and moon combination is not one that creates someone who is overly ambitious.

This is why those who have this sun and moon combination are usually a type 9 personality but heavily lean on the 8 wing. The rising sign and the house placements are not overly relevant. However, some can influence them to lean on the 8 wing heavier than others such as having a rising sign in Capricorn or a full 10th house.

Sagittarius Sun and a Moon in Scorpio

Those that have this sun and moon combination are the ultimate go-getters, know exactly how to get what they want and need, are clever, shrewd, and have a great sense for business. They can be aggressive but are also sensitive at times. Those with this sun and moon combination are either a type 3 or a type 8. Those with earth and water signs with the exception of Scorpio as rising signs may lean more towards a type 3 as they are more focused on their own achievements but less when it comes to controlling others - unless there is a competitive threat.

However, with those that have air and fire signs as rising signs as well as Scorpio may be more of a type 8 as they can be quite domineering and far more aggressive with those who pose as threats.

Sagittarius Sun with a Sagittarius Moon

Those with this sun and moon combination are the types that have so much fiery energy that they are on the go, can be impulsive, and are always looking forward to the next best thing. They tend to exhaust themselves because they are constantly on the go. However, they will assume responsibility if they need to clear something up. And they will be more in control if they see that something is poorly managed or if something is half done. They expect others to live up to their standards and are not overly sensitive to the feelings of others.

Those that have this sun and moon combination are a type 7 but will heavily lean on an 8 wing. And those that have Aries, Scorpio, or Capricorn as their rising signs and a full 10th house may be more of a type 8 but would lie heavily on their 7 wing. They are far more controlling with those placements.

Sagittarius Sun with a Capricorn Moon

Those that have this sun and moon combination are highly ambitious and have a strong need to keep a prestigious reputation, and are excellent with handling business affairs. Yet at the same time, their Sagittarian influence keeps them from being too serious as they still have a great deal of optimism and have an appreciation for culture. Those that have this sun and moon placement will be a type 3 personality.

Those that have Cancer, Virgo, or Libra as rising signs and/or has a strong 6th or 7th house may lean more on the 2 wing as they would be happy to help others. Those that have water signs other than Cancer, as well as air signs as rising signs with full water houses, may lean more towards the 4 wing. They would be a little more emotional, sensitive, possibly eccentric, and even artistic.

Sagittarius Sun and an Aquarius Moon

Those that have this sun and moon combination are highly expressive, advocating, proactive, and at the same time are quite peaceful and friendly. They are highly influential and assume many leadership roles. Those that have this sun and moon combination are a type 9 because of their desire for peace but do heavily lean on their 8 wing because of the fact that even though they would be a type 9 they are quite grounded and will speak up for something that is quite important.

The rising signs and house placements don't have a huge effect, and many of those with this sun and moon combination do end up going into politics, organizations, the community, or can be excellent motivational speakers.

Sun in Sagittarius and a Moon in Pisces

Those with this sun and moon combination are highly idealistic, don't want to get into conflicts, don't tend to put their foot down when they really should, are extremely kind and tolerant. They do recognize the truth because they are highly intuitive but tend to put up with more than they should. Those with this sun and moon combination are a type 9 personality.

Those that have fire or air signs as rising signs, in addition to Capricorn and/or a stellium in their 1st, 7th, or 10th house may lean more towards an 8 wing which will ground them more. With that said, they will have an easier time speaking up for what they believe in. Those that have Taurus or Virgo as rising signs and has a strong 6th house may lean more towards the 1 wing which will also help them stay more organized and down to earth as well.

That sums up the Sagittarius sun and moon combinations that determine the personality type on the Enneagram model. In the next chapter, the Capricorn sun and moon combinations will be examined as well as the personality types of those with those combos will be determined.

Capricorn Sun And Moon Combinations And Personality Types

NOW, IT IS time to look at the personality types of those who have their Sun in Capricorn mixed with the moons in the 12 signs. You may assume that based on the nature of the Capricorn that they would either be 6's, 3's, or 8's. Some of that may be true but others are not, just like with the previous signs that were examined. Let's check it out now and see what type of personality the Capricorn sun and 12 moon combinations bring.

Capricorn Sun and an Aries Moon

Those that have this sun and moon combination are going to be very ambitious and prestige is quite important to them. They are prepared to work very hard and also have a good sense about business, so they have a strong drive to succeed and will. They are quite shrewd and are excellent self-starters as well. It is not a surprise that those that have this sun and moon combination have a type 3 personality.

Those that have Cancer or Libra as their rising signs and/or has a strong 6th, 7th or 11th house will lean more towards the 2 wing as they will be willing to help others succeed and are more compassionate. Those that have Aquarius or Pisces as their rising signs and have full water houses will likely lean more towards the 4 wing as they may be more eccentric, dramatic, and artistic.

Capricorn Sun and a Taurus Moon

Those with this sun and moon combination are extremely down to earth, fixed in their ideas, and are professional by nature. They are highly determined to succeed as well, and once they make up their minds to do something, they do it, and they can tackle any challenge that is thrown at them. They are not harsh in nature and if they are critical of anyone, they are quite gentle about how they convey the criticism.

Those with this sun and moon combination are a type 3 personality, or maybe a type 8 with a very strong 9 wing, or may even be a type 9 but heavily lays on the 8 wing only for the sake of not wanting to get into conflicts but are determined for what they believe in.

However, those that have Cancer, Libra, or Pisces as rising signs and/or has full water houses may be more of a type 9 personality that leans heavily on the 8 wing.

Capricorn Sun and a Gemini Moon

Those with this sun and moon placement are very expressive and ambitious. They have a way with words and are quick thinkers. They have their own ways to express themselves, as they can be somewhat eccentric in their ways of expression and can be anxious at times. They tend to be self-confident but at the same time, can be self-conscious. This sun and moon placement are excellent for writing or for any marketing or advertising field.

Those that have this sun and moon placement are either a 3 type personality that leans on the 4 wing or a type 4 personality that leans on the 3 wing. They are ambitious but at the same time emotional and can be quite individualistic.

Those that have water signs as rising signs and/or has full water houses may be more of a type 4 personality that lays heavily on the 3 wing.

Capricorn Sun with a Cancer Moon

Those that have this sun and moon combination are quite sensitive and can easily pick up intuitively on whether or not something is trustworthy or not. Many times they even question their intuition. They prefer to be homebodies and place a big emphasis on their families. They are very introspective and may read into things too much. Those that have this sun and moon placement are a type 6 personality.

However, those that have fire signs as rising signs and/or has a full 5th, 7th, or 11th house may lean more towards the 7 wing and be slightly more extroverted and adventurous. Those that have air signs as rising signs and have a full 3rd, 9th, or 11th houses will lean more towards the 5 wing and be more observant and be pacified by intellectual stimulation.

Capricorn Sun and a Leo Moon

Those that have this sun and moon combination are highly ambitious but are diplomatic. And they are highly competitive but go about how they compete in a quiet manner as they never want to make a fuss. That is not cool to them. They want to be at the top and be prestigious and have an excellent reputation. Making a fuss about what they want in an overt way is not cool to them. Those that have this sun and moon type are a hardcore type 3 personality.

They may subtly lean on the 2 wing if they have Cancer, Virgo, or Libra as rising signs and/or has a full 6th, 7th, or 11th house as they are more willing to be helpful. However, this is a powerful sun and moon combination so this would be subtle. They would learn more heavily on their 4 wing if they have Scorpio, Aquarius, or Pisces rising and/or has full water houses. They would still be a strong type 3 but would be expressive in their own way, and somewhat more eccentric.

Capricorn Sun and a Moon in Virgo

Those that have this sun and moon combination are extremely reserved, go by the book, are not changeable, and have a hard time making decisions. They have a logical way of thinking at the same time due to being highly analytical when it comes to anything that doesn't involve them in a personal way that would get into the way of their emotions. That said they can easily look at things that don't involve them objectively. They thrive on intellectual stimulation and anything that is academic.

Those that have this sun and moon placement may be either a type 5 personality that lies on the 6 wing or a type 6 personality that lies on the 5 wing. Those that have Cancer or Libra rising and/or has a full 7th or 11th house may be a type 5 that lies on a 6 wing as they are heavily reserved and keep to themselves but want to have relationships. Those that have Aries, Virgo, or

Aquarius rising and/or has a full 3rd or 9th house may be a type 6 and lies heavily on the 5 wing. They have an easier time being introspective and less anxious than a core 6.

Capricorn Sun and a Libra Moon

Those that have this sun and moon combination are not typical Capricorns as they are impulsive, very friendly, but detached, and is quite suspicious of people's motives even if there is no reason to be that way. They tend to look at the negative side of things before looking at anything positive which is a good thing in order to analyze flaws that need to be fixed when it comes to work or business. They prefer material things over people and are not into relationships. Those who have this sun and moon combination are either type 7 personalities that lie heavily on the 6 wing or are type 6 personalities that lie heavily on the 7 wing.

Those that have water signs as rising signs or earth signs and/or has full water houses would be a type 6 due to their anxious nature but would have the urge to try new things and be somewhat adventurous. Those that have fire or air signs as rising signs and/or has a full 1st, 7th, 10th, or 11th house may be more a type 7 personality who is far more adventurous but leans on the 6 wing which will cause them to want to be with others and will ground them somewhat.

Capricorn Sun and a Scorpio Moon

Those that have this sun and moon combination are highly ambitious, have a strong inner drive, and is well respected. The expression is done in a quiet way, and this individual is intense on the inside but is also reserved. This means that if they don't approve of something, they make it known without making a fuss. Even though those with this sun and moon combination are reasonable, they are also quite inflexible. Those that have this sun and moon combination are a type 3 personality but heavily lean on the 4 wing.

They are ambitious and very driven but have unique ways of expressing that and they, in fact, are quite quiet on the outside but within they have plenty going on. The rising sign and house placements are not too relevant with this sun and moon combination.

Capricorn Sun and a Sagittarius Moon

Those that have this sun and moon combination are extremely outgoing, adventurous, love to travel, and have a variety of interests and love to be involved in many activities. But they also are diplomatic, shrewd, and sincere. Those that have this sun and moon combination have a type 7 personality but lean on their 8 wing regardless of the rising sign and house placements.

They have the heart of a typical Sagittarius but are kept grounded for the most part by their Capricorn Sun.

Capricorn Sun and a Capricorn Moon

This sun and moon combination basically screams perfection. Those that have this sun and moon placement are highly rigid, have high expectations of themselves and of others, and will not accept anything that is less. They only want to achieve the best and nothing else will do, however, they are dependable. Those who have this sun and moon placement are the typical type 1 personality.

Those that have Cancer or Libra as rising signs and/or has a full 7th or 11th house may be more thoughtful and helpful and will lean more on the 2 wing. Those that have mutable signs as their rising signs may lean towards the 9 wing as they are still rigid but will be able to adapt to things better and relax a little more.

Capricorn Sun and an Aquarius Moon

Those with this sun and moon combination are quite progressive, sincere, and has the desire to be involved in many different things.

They can be quite original and creative but are also seen as social climbers as status is very important. This is why those with this sun and moon combination are a type 3 but lean heavily onto the 4 wing.

It doesn't matter what the rising signs and house placements are. These individuals are naturally ambitious but are creative with how they take actions, and unique in general.

Capricorn Sun and a Pisces Moon

Those that have this sun and moon combination are quite influenced by outside environments but are also ambitious in their own way. However, the Pisces aspect can erase the firmness that comes with Capricorn and can be quite sympathetic instead. They are quite honest and never would trick anyone into anything. They are not overly materialistic but can end up having some strong expectations. Sometimes they become upset if they have not been reciprocated in the way they had liked if they went out of their way to help others, especially with family.

Those that have this placement can either be a type 2 or a type 9 personality. Those that have a type 2 personality would have water or earth signs as their rising signs and/or would have full water houses. They would be the ones to give everything of themselves but will become very upset if they are not reciprocated. Those that have fire or air signs as rising signs would be more of a type 9 and may even lean more towards an 8 wing as they still are quite peaceful but would not hold back if they were angered and could explode potentially.

That concludes the Capricorn sun and moon combinations as now we are going to examine the second last sign of the zodiac, Aquarius and its 12 different moon sign combinations. That is how the personality types will be determined for those who have the Aquarius sun sign.

Aquarius Sun And Moon Combinations And Personality Types

NOW WE ARE in the Aquarius Sun section and it is time to examine the personality types that result from each Aquarius Sun and moon combinations. You may be thinking that those who have an Aquarius Sun are the type to sit back, observe, and stay detached and that would make them an automatic type 5. However, if you have learned something from reading the previous chapters on the other sun and moon combinations, you will see how that in itself cannot be generalized. The same applies to Aquarius! Let's go over the 12 moon signs mixed with the Aquarius sun right now!

Aquarius Sun and an Aries Moon

Those that have this sun and moon combination are extremely independent, pushy, and absolutely hate being controlled at all costs. They would not work well under any type of supervision and would only be at their best when they are their own boss. They also are quite detached by nature and would much rather be alone, and in control as well. There is no doubt that those with this sun and moon sign combination are a type 8 personality.

Those that have their rising signs in Cancer, Libra or Pisces and/or has a full 7th or 11th house would lean more towards a 9 wing where they would be less pushy, more compassionate, and would overall be softened. Those that have Leo or Sagittarius as rising signs and/or has a full 5th or 9th house would lean more towards the 7 wing and be more adventurous and less rigid.

Aquarius Sun with a Taurus Moon

Those with this sun and moon combination are the type that do not have much of a will to succeed or climb the ladder. They are also not the type to unload their anxieties or concerns onto others but are always there to listen to others and will even drop everything they do in order to be there for everyone else. They like being around others but at the same time do keep a distance. They are quite passive but at the same time are stubborn about only the things that are important to them.

Those that have this sun and moon combination are a type 9 personality. However, those that have Aries, Scorpio, or Capricorn and/or that have a full 1st or 10th house will lean more towards the 8 wing. They are the ones that are more grounded and ambitious and will speak up if they are very upset. Those that have Virgo rising and/or a full 6th house will lean more towards the 1 wing where they will be more organized and analytical.

Aquarius Sun with a Gemini Moon

Those that have this sun and moon combination are idealistic, never stay in the moment, and jump from one thing to the next. They are extremely creative but they can struggle with a short attention span. They may be ambitious with one thing for one moment but then they will end up finding something better and drop what they were doing. This is why those with this sun and moon combination are a type 7 personality.

Those however that have Cancer, Virgo, Libra or Aquarius as rising signs and/or has a strong 6th, 7th or 11th house would lean more towards the 6 wing which would help them in regards to teamwork and relationships. And those that have Aries, Scorpio, or Capricorn rising and/or have a full 1st or 10th house would lean more towards the 8 wing which would ground them and make them more ambitious and focused.

Sun in Aquarius and a Moon in Cancer

Those that have this sun and moon combination take on more of the Cancerian trait because the Sun is in its detriment in Cancer. That means those who have this combination are going to be very sensitive, receptive, and be the ones to help others, and will value home and family. That means those that have this sun and moon combination could be either a type 2 or a type 6.

Those that have Cancer or Libra as rising signs and/or has a full 5th or 7th house would be a type 2, and perhaps the earth signs as rising signs would lean them towards a 3 wing which would make them more ambitious which would be good for business. Those that have water signs as rising signs, as well as Aquarius and/or, has full water houses would be a type 6 due to their anxious and suspicious nature due to being extremely sensitive - but detached due to fear of getting hurt from getting too close.

Aquarius Sun and a Leo Moon

Those that have this sun and moon combination possess similar traits to the Aquarius Sun and Taurus Moon combo. They are fixed in their ideas but are also the type to want to please, do not want conflict, are sympathetic, are too kind to a fault, and they want peace. They are most definitely a type 9 personality.

Those that have Aries, Scorpio, or Capricorn as their rising signs and/or has a strong 1st or 10th house will lean more towards the 8 wing which will help them be more ambitious, grounded, and they will speak up if something needs to be said. Those that have Vigo rising and/or has a full 6th house will lean more towards the 1 wing where they will have higher standards for themselves and be more organized.

Aquarius Sun and a Virgo Moon

Those with this sun and moon combination are logical, excellent analyzers, excellent advisors, intuitive are friendly but at the same time are detached and aloof. They have a scientific way of thinking, and they can have a perfectionist attitude as well. Those that have this sun and moon combination are either a type 1 or a type 5.

Those that have their rising signs in earth signs and/or has a full 6th house will be type 1 as they will have the ultimate perfectionist attitude. Perhaps Cancer or Libra rising and/or has a full 7th house may lean them towards the 2 wing which will make them more helpful and social to a degree.

Those that have Gemini or Aquarius as rising signs and/or has a full 3rd or 9th house will make them more of a type 5 personality. However, those that have Scorpio or Pisces as rising signs and/or has full water houses may either make them lean towards a 4 wing or may even be a type 4 leaning on the 5 wing. They would be eccentric, aloof, but highly emotional and creative.

Aquarius Sun with a Libra Moon

Those that have this sun and moon combination are known to be quite friendly, but flighty and quite inconsistent. They want to look for the next best thing and are the types to leave projects undone. They have many friends and marriage and relationships are important but are not the type to be committed and to settle down. Those that have this sun and moon combination are a type 7 personality.

However, those that have Cancer, Virgo, or Libra rising and/or has a strong 7th house will lean more towards the 6 wing and be able to be more committed with relationships. Those that have Scorpio or Capricorn rising and/or has a full 10th house will lean more towards the 8 wing which will provide them more direction, ambition, and practicality.

Aquarius Sun with a Scorpio Moon

Those that have this sun and moon combination are very rigid, independent, and have their own high standards. They are not just judgemental of others but are very judgemental of themselves if they are not 'perfect'. They have a hard time with any kind of chaos and imperfection and lack of control. They can be great leaders as well, and want to be in control but not in an overly aggressive kind of way. Those who have this sun and moon combination are a type 1 personality.

However, those that have Cancer, Virgo, or Libra as rising signs and/or has a strong 7th or 11th house will lean more towards the 2 wing and will be more cooperative and helpful with others. Those that have Leo, Sagittarius, or Aquarius as rising signs and/or has a strong 5th or 9th house will lean more towards the 9 wing as they will be more relaxed and less rigid.

Aquarius Sun with a Sagittarius Moon

Those who have this sun and moon combination are active, expressive, original, creative, honest, and wants to help those in need. That means they have a strong humanitarian side to them. They are very friendly and helpful but will not tolerate any type of sham or deception at all. They also are dreamers even though they have a logical side. They like to get things done quickly and have an innovative approach to how things are done as they can easily think outside of the box. Those that have this sun and moon combination are either a type 5 but heavily lean on the 6 wing or a type 5 that heavily leans on the 4 wing.

Those that have Aries, Gemini, Leo, Sagittarius, Aquarius, or Pisces as rising signs and/or has full 3rd, 5th, or 9th or the water houses may lean more towards the 4 wing which will increase their creativity but would be far more dramatic and emotional in their approach. and would embrace their uniqueness. Those that have Cancer, Virgo, or Libra as their rising signs and/or has a strong 6th or 7th house would lean more towards the 6 wing which would increase their desire to socialize and be an excellent problem-solver to help others. They would be more cooperative in teamwork settings.

Aquarius Sun with a Capricorn Moon

Those that have this sun and moon placement are focused, professional, and are excellent leaders, and only want lead and never want to follow. However, they can be cold but they also have a soft side to them as they have a strong humanitarian nature. They want to be the leaders but will be there to help others if they are in need. That is why those that have this sun and moon placement are either an 8 type personality that leans heavily on the 9 wing, or a 1 type personality that leans heavily on the 2 wing.

Those that have fixed signs as rising signs along with Virgo and/ or has a strong 6th house will be likely the type 1 personality that leans heavily on the 2 wing. They are more about perfection instead of wanting to be in control of others around them. Those that have fire signs, as well as Capricorn as rising signs and/or a full 1st or 10th house, will be a type 8 as they are more concerned about control but have a strong humanitarian streak as to why they would lean heavily on the 9 wing.

Aquarius Sun with an Aquarius Moon

Those that have this sun and moon combination are extremely detached, stubborn, are the true observers, and thrive on intellectual stimulation but have a humanitarian and an eccentric way about them as they are a double Aquarius. Those that have this sun and moon combo would most definitely be a type 5 and, in some cases, they would heavily lean towards the 4 wing. Especially if they have fire or water signs as their rising signs and/or have full water houses or believed it or not, a full 10th house. They want to make their uniqueness known and want to have that reputation as being different and unique.

Aquarius Sun with a Pisces Moon

Those who have this sun and moon combination are extremely dreamy, intuitive, and are highly imaginative. They do not have strong leadership skills and live their lives through study and creativity. They absolutely love intellectual stimulation as well and would be the true definition as the ultimate Bohemian. Those that have this sun and moon combination would be a type 4 that would heavily lean towards the 5 wing which is what the Bohemian is known for.

The rising signs and house placements are not overly relevant with this sun and moon combination. This concludes the Aquarius Sun with the 12 moon combinations that determines the personality type on the Enneagram model. The next chapter will cover the Pisces sun and moon combinations that will determine the personality types.

Pisces Sun And Moon Combinations And Personality Types

NOW WE ARE going to be examining the sun and moon combinations of the last sun sign in the zodiac, Pisces. And it is a known fact that Pisces is associated with dreaminess, lack of boundaries and reality, creativity, and intuition. That would automatically make you think that those who have a sun in Pisces would be a type 9 personality. That may be true in some cases, but just as you have learned in the other sun and moon combinations, that is not necessarily going to be the case. Let's take a look at the sun and moon combinations of the last sign in the zodiac, and determine the personality type of the Enneagram model that results from it.

Pisces Sun and an Aries Moon

This sun and moon combination creates an individual that has a need to be recognized for their accomplishments, and they are also quite ambitious due to the Arian drive, they are also quite independent and have a strong desire to acquire knowledge. Once they have a strong desire to go after something, then they do take action to go after it in their own unique way. Those that have this sun and moon combination are a type 3 but lean heavily on a 4 wing due to their need to be expressive in a unique way, and they can be quite emotional and artistic.

The rising sign and house placement are not overly relevant. The only thing that is possible is that those that have water signs as rising signs and/or has full water houses may be more of a type 4 personality and lie heavily on a 3 wing.

Pisces Sun with a Taurus Moon

Those that have this sun and moon combination are highly agreeable, sensitive, and don't ever want to hurt the other person's feelings, and they don't like conflicts for the most part. However, they will make themselves clear if they do not approve of something that affects them in a personal way and can be blunt about it. They also can be quite stubborn due to the nature of the moon sign about certain things that would be important to them or that they strongly believe.

Those that have this sun and moon combination are a type 9 but would lie heavily on the 8 wing. Those that have earth signs as rising signs, as well as Aries and Scorpio and/or has a strong 1st or 10th house may be more into the 8 wing than the others. However, they still want peace regardless. They would just be more grounded, practical, and less shy about conflicts.

Pisces Sun and a Moon in Gemini

Those that have this sun and moon combination are not overly grounded, indecisive, but at the same time can be stubborn, and do not want to hurt anyone intentionally. In fact, they really hate the idea of hurting anyone and will avoid anything that could potentially cause any pain. They are stubborn but notorious for changing their minds quickly and are not always reliable when it comes to finishing important tasks. Those that have this sun and moon combination are a type 9 personality.

However, those that have Capricorn as well as Aries or Scorpio as their rising signs and/or, has full 1st or 10th houses will lean more towards the 8 wing as they will be more practical, ambitious, and will be more willing to focus on something they want to go after. Those that have Taurus, Virgo, or Aquarius and/or has a full 6th house will lean more towards the 1 wing and they would prefer to be more organized and will have higher standards of themselves and of others.

Pisces Sun and a Cancer Moon

Those that have this sun and moon combination are very sensitive, intuitive, and extremely empathetic. However, they are also extremely disciplined, driven, and will tackle any task with great intensity because they will only accept the best efforts from themselves. They will not associate with others who they strongly sense are bad news. Those that have this sun and moon combination are a type 1 but heavily lean on 2 wing because of their extremely sensitive nature.

However, those that have water signs as rising signs as well as Libra, and a full 7th or 11th house will be more of a type 2 and will rely heavily on the 1 wing.

Pisces Sun and a Leo Moon

Those that have this sun and moon combination are the ultimate people-pleasers because they do not want to deal with any conflict and will frequently give in to the wishes of others even if they are not at ease with what they are asked to do. They are very warm and caring as well. And those that have this sun and moon combination are a type 9 personality.

However, those that have Capricorn as well as Aries or Scorpio as their rising signs and/or has full 1st or 10th houses will lean more towards the 8 wing as they will be more practical, ambitious, and will be more willing to focus on something they want to go after. Those that have Taurus, Virgo, or Aquarius and/or has a full 6th house will lean more towards the 1 wing and they would prefer to be more organized and will have higher standards of themselves and of others.

Pisces sun with a Virgo Moon

Those that have this sun and moon combination are highly analytical and yet quite intuitive, and tend to keep to themselves more often and would rather observe life from the outside than to participate. However, they are also down to earth and that means if they have to deal with business or any life situation that is questionable such as having to sign contracts, they would rely on their intuition in addition to logic before making agreements. Those that have this sun and moon combination need to be intellectually stimulated and are known to be ambitious but don't really take themselves overly seriously and rarely end up meeting their goals.

Those that have this sun and moon combination are a type 5, and those that have water signs as rising signs and/or have full water houses will lean towards the 4 wing which would make them more emotional, artistic, and even expressive in their own unique way. Those that have Libra or Aquarius or sometimes Cancer as rising signs would be leaning more towards the 6 wing and/or has a full 6th or 7th house as they may be loners but still desire companionship and value teamwork.

Pisces Sun and a Libra Moon

Those that have this sun and moon combination are extremely dreamy, intuitive, and are highly imaginative as well. They do not like conflicts at all costs and have a fine appreciation for the arts. They are the type that would be there for those who are in need. Those who have this sun and moon combination would mostly be the 9 type personality but would in some cases be more of a 4 type.

Those that have full water houses and/or has a rising sign in Gemini, Leo, Virgo, or Scorpio may be more of a 4 as they would be more dramatic, eccentric, and be more self-absorbed and focusing on their own issues. However, those who have Aries or Capricorn as their rising signs and/or has a full 1st or 10th house would be a type 9 that heavily leans on an 8 wing as they would be more grounded, practical, ambitious, and would not be afraid to speak up if necessary.

Pisces Sun and a Scorpio Moon

This sun and moon combination brings out a very sensitive type who is not afraid to express their feelings and themselves no matter how awkward. They are powerful observers and are highly intuitive. They can be ambitious if there is a strong need for them to be and have some strong plans in order to reach a goal but they are quite secretive about how they go by it. They are often too moody in order to have stable relationships but it can happen depending on other placements in their horoscopes.

Those that have this sun and moon combination are a type 4, and those that have earth signs as rising signs as well as Aries, Gemini, and sometimes Scorpio and/or has a strong 1st or 10th house will lean heavily on the 3 wing as they are more ambitious and goal-oriented. Those that have Virgo, Aquarius or any of the water signs as rising signs and have a strong 3rd or 9th house will lean heavily on the 5 wing and live more of a Bohemian lifestyle.

Pisces Sun with a Moon in Sagittarius

Those that have this sun and moon combination are always looking forward to the next best thing, are not practical, and are quite dreamy. They have a hard time living in the moment as they are always looking to experience some type of adventure and are strong dreamers. They are extremely idealistic and have a tendency to take on too much, and spread themselves thin. Those that have this sun and moon combination are a type 7.

However, those that have Gemini, Cancer, Virgo, Libra, or Aquarius rising sign and/or has a strong 7th or 11th house will lean more towards the 6 wing and be more sociable and less adventurous. Those that have Aries, Scorpio, or Capricorn as their rising signs and/or has a strong 10th house will lean more towards the 8 wing and will be more practical and ambitious, and goal-oriented.

Pisces Sun with a Capricorn Moon

Those that have this sun and moon combination are sensitive and understanding towards the needs of others and yet at the same time are quite ambitious, organized, and goal-oriented. They strive to be good leaders and are practical about how they go by that but are never arrogant and while they work on achieving their goals they are sensitive to the needs of others.

Those that have this sun and moon combination are a type 3 but heavily lean on the 2 wing regardless of their rising sign and house placements. They want to help others in need but are still striving to be the best.

Pisces Sun with an Aquarius Moon

This individual with this sun and moon combination are true humanitarians and want to be peaceful around others. They are quite friendly but at the same time have a strong desire to be independent and find their way to success. They are quite intuitive and are able to sniff out the bullshit easily and call it out if necessary. They are overall cooperative and peaceful but do not like anything that is dull and want some type of excitement. And they are highly dedicated once they know what they want to do with their lives and will achieve it.

Those that have this sun and moon combination are a type 9 but will lean heavily on the 8 wing regardless of rising sign and house placement. They are peacemakers and keepers for the most part but will also go after what they need and want without any problem.

Pisces Sun and a Pisces Moon

Those that have this sun and moon combination are highly sensitive and also withdrawn. They only want to maintain relationships with those who they are close to and never look for other friends unless they are seeking a relationship for reasons of their own. They are highly intuitive and quite observant. They are also extremely artistic and creative. They may appear eccentric and can be so withdrawn that they may be inaccessible but they are always observing and learning through intuition. If they seem closed off it is because they are working hard on processing situations.

Those that have this sun and moon combination are a type 5 that leans heavily on the 4 wing. They are true hermits but are quite emotional and have an appreciation for the arts of any type.

That concludes the Pisces Sun and Moon combinations, which also concludes all of the 144 sun and moon combinations that indicate the personality type through the Enneagram model. However, if you have read your own sun and moon combination and it doesn't quite resonate, there may be a strong reason for that.

There are cases when a planet that is in the first house, especially if it is very close to the Ascendant would be a better indicator of the personality type represented in the Enneagram model more strongly than the sun and moon combination. However, no matter what, the sun and moon combination still holds a lot of importance. Because if you are one of those types that has a planet in the first house that represents who you really are, then the sun and moon combination in your case could part of the Tritype.

And, before the Tritypes and instincts of the Enneagram are covered, let's cover the personality types that may be the dominant one if there is a planet in the first house that is close to the Ascendant - in the next chapter.

Planets In The First House Representing The Personality Types

YOU JUST READ about the 144 sun and moon combinations and the personality type on the Enneagram model that it matches. However, in some cases, that may not completely resonate and in those cases, it would be likely due to the fact that the personality type is represented by the planet that is in the 1st house which would be the dominant one. Not the rising sign! The planet. And since the 1st house represents your overall personality, then any planet that is in that house regardless of how it is aspected to other planets may be the very thing that indicates your personality type.

And in that situation, the sun and moon combination that matches a personality type on the Enneagram model would be likely a Tritype instead. Tritypes and instincts will be discussed in the next chapter. However, in this chapter, we will cover the planets in the first house regardless of the sign that could have more of an influence on your personality type. Now, let's look at the planets in the first house and see what main personality type you have as a result:

- **Sun in the first house** - Those that have Sun in the first house will magnify their importance, and will be the ones to be in the center of the spotlight, and will want to be the best at whatever they do. Let's face it, they are show-offs and those with a 1st house Sun would likely be a type 3 personality. They most definitely will be highly competitive and strive to be the best at whatever is the most important to them.
- **Moon in the first house** - Those who have the Moon in their first house are natural nurturers and will be there to help others, and take care of them as well. They are also highly

emotional and it is safe to say that those who have a first house moon regardless of the sign will be a type 2.

- **Mercury in the first house** - Those that have Mercury in the first house are quite analytical, conversational, have a tendency to think too much, and may possibly even have a perfectionist attitude. Those that have Mercury in the first house may either be a type 1 or a type 5, which depends on the other placements. That is because Mercury rules both Virgo and Gemini. If there is more Virgo influence in the overall chart such as having more planets in earth signs and/or a 6th house stellium, then the individual would be more of a type 1. If the individual has a lot of air in the chart and/or has a full 3rd house or 9th house, then the individual would be more of a thinker and observer type. That means the individual could be more of a type 5 personality, and if he or she prefers to socialize but likes to observe and need intellectual stimulation, then that would only mean that he or she would lean on a 6 wing due to other influences in the chart.

- **Venus in the first house** - Those that have Venus in the first house will be the types to want to please others, and they will only want peace and beauty is very important to them. They enjoy the fine physical things in life because of comfort, as those with Venus in the first house want comfort. That means those who have this placement will likely be a type 9.

- **Mars in the first house** - Mars in the first house creates someone who is passionate, energetic, and can be aggressive and even controlling. Those that have this placement can be a type 8 personality or may be a type 3. The difference would be is whether or not the social houses would be full such as a full 3rd, 7th, or 11th house. If those houses are full then this means that they know how to win others over and care very much as well how others see them. They want to be the best at what they do and will focus their energies on that so that would make them more of a type 3. Otherwise, they would be a type 8 and would care more about control. Either way, those that have Mars in the first house are powerful leaders.

- **Jupiter in the first house** - Those that have Jupiter in the first house will be quite expansive, adventurous, will always be looking forward to the next moment and have a great deal of enthusiasm. Those that have Jupiter in the first house will be a type 7 because that is what Jupiter represents!
- **Saturn in the first house** - Those that have Saturn in the first house may be suspicious, fearful, and anxiety-ridden due to fearing the worst thing that could possibly happen. They are not at ease and restrict themselves from many opportunities. Those with Saturn in the first house needs their comfort zone, and that means they will be a type 6 because of their fearful nature.
- **Uranus in the first house** - Those that have Uranus in the first house are introspective, inventive, need intellectual stimulation, and can be eccentric, and are detached. Those that have this placement can be a type 5 easily.
- **Neptune in the first house** - Those that have Neptune in the first house are highly emotional and irrational, and are incredibly creative, intuitive, imaginative, and are not grounded in reality. They would rather live in a fairy tale than to deal with the painful reality and that is why those who have this placement would be a type 4.
- **Pluto in the first house** - Those that have Pluto in the first house are controlling, powerful, and will always be the one to lead and never to be the one to follow. They can also be quite protective of those they love. Those who have this placement are a type 8.

This would hold more truth as well if the planets were in their home signs or exalted signs in the first house. If they are in their detriment or in fall, then their sun and moon combination would likely represent their dominant personality. However, the wings that they would lean on would also depend on other factors in their personal chart. Additionally, whether or not they bring out the best of each personality type would also depend on how well their home planets (in their first houses) aspect to other planets in their charts.

Now that you know that there are other influences in the natal chart other than the sun and moon combination that can represent the personality type on the Enneagram model, you will learn something else. The Tritypes and the instincts. That means the personality type that you have been reading about is the main one. However, there are tritypes as well, and instincts and the next chapter will cover more information on that.

The Instincts And Tritypes® In The Enneagram Model

THERE IS MORE to the Enneagram model other than the main personality types, the arrows, and the wings. You also have the centers and the instincts which were taught by Enneagram researcher, teacher and coach Katherine Chernick Fauvre of Katherine Fauvre Consulting. Katherine also co-founded Enneagram Explorations with David W. Fauvre who shares the Tritype® copyright with Katherine. As you know the Latin prefix tri means three. And combining that term with type is what represents the 2 other personalities that people would have as well that are not the dominant ones.

With that said, even if the sun and moon combination brings out a personality type that is not likely your dominant one, then it is likely a component of your Tritype. Enneagram researcher and coach Katherine Chernick Fauvre conducted research in the mid-1990s to uncover this aspect of the Enneagram as the two other personalities that you would have would be influential in some ways.

Think about as well, how planets in houses and the aspects they make to one another have an influence on you. It all ties together. Now, in order to make this clear, you first need to understand the 3 instincts before delving into the Tritypes which are also referred to as the centers in the Enneagram Model. And by the way, it is not the same thing as the wings, this is completely different.

The Centers Or The Instincts Of The Enneagram

The 3 centers of the Enneagram model or instincts is what rules 3 different personality types. And they are the thinking center, the feeling center, and the body center which was established by Oscar Ichazo. Let's go over these now:

The Thinking Center

The thinking center is also referred to as the head, center of intelligence or mental center of the Enneagram which is where fear also stems from, as well as your ability to be analytical, imaginative, think, predict, plan and assess in general. The personality types that this center consists of are types 5, 6, and 7.

The Feeling Center

The feeling center is also referred to as the heart center which is the emotional area. This is what rules your connections, feelings, worth, relationships, your ability to bond, but also rules shame, grief, and sadness. The personality types that this center consists of are types 2, 3, and 4.

The Body Center

The body center is also referred to as the center of movement, personal power, boundaries, respect, lovability, action-taking, relate to the physical world and comfort. However, this area rules anger, resentment, impatience, and resistance. The personality types that this center consists of are types 8, 9 and 1.

What does this all mean? This means that your overall personality consists of three Enneagram Types, not just one and that you have a type from each center of attention which creates your Tritype. One type is always dominant. This means your dominant personality type would be from any of the centers and that you also have other 2 personality types from the 2 other centers which are more subtle but still very influential. They are less dominant than the primary type but work as co types.

In other words, if your dominant personality type is 4 which would be from the feeling center, you would have another type from the thinking center which could be either 5, 6, or 7. And, you would have another personality type from the body center which could be either 8, 9, or 1. You cannot have 2 or 3 personality types from the same center. You have each one from the 3 centers, with one of them being the dominant type.

I am a type 4, which is my dominant type and my Tritype is 459. My dominant is 4, and 5 is my type from the thinking center, and 9 is my 9 from the body center. According to Fauvre, that makes me the contemplative type and that is so true. This means that I tend to go into deep (which is what the 4 represents), thinking (which is the 5) and it can be prolonged where I would take my time figuring things out (which is where the 9 type comes in). And someone who has the same Tritype may have 9 more dominant than 5 where they would take even longer to process thoughts and find deeper meaning and would have the Tritype of 495 instead. It all boils down how they navigate their surroundings. This is why she refers to this Tritype as *The Contemplative.*

The same would apply to those whose dominant type would be 5 or 9 as well. That just means the numbers would be in different directions. That just means that someone who has a dominant 5 type could be a 549 or a 594, or someone who has a dominant 9 type could be a 945 or a 954 would also be *The Contemplative,* according to Fauvre.

Another example of the Tritype which Katherine Chernick Fauvre had shared on her website is the 935 Tritype which she refers to as *The Thinker.* The 9 type is dominant which would cause the individual to appear soft and peaceful, however with the Tritype 3 in the picture - the individual would come off as being professional and would be more expedient. And then with the Type 5 also in the picture, this would cause the person to be more remote, concealed, observant, and analytical while taking in information. Picture that type of person. Now you would understand how Fauvre refers to those who have this Tritype as *The Thinker.*

Now, let's briefly look at 27 archetypical Tritypes by Katherine Chernick Fauvre. If you find that your sun and moon combination don't resonate with that type being dominant, then chances are you will find that it resonates with a part of your Tritype component.

Here are Fauvre's 27 archetypical Tritypes which come right from her website, in addition to her titles that go along with them due to the fact that they best describe the corresponding Tritype. The brief descriptions are quite self-explanatory which means there is no need for elaboration:

The Tritypes are credited by and found through the work of Katherine Chernick Fauvre and David W. Fauvre, MA

125, 152, 215, 251, 512, 521-The Mentor
126, 162, 216, 261, 612, 621-The Supporter
127, 172, 217, 271, 712, 721-The Teacher
135, 153, 315, 351, 513, 531-The Technical Expert
136, 163, 316, 361, 613, 631-The Taskmaster
137, 173, 317, 371, 713, 731-The Systems Builder
145, 154, 415, 451, 514, 541-The Researcher
146, 164, 416, 461, 614, 641-The Philosopher
147, 174, 417, 471, 714, 741-The Visionary
258, 285, 528, 582, 825, 852-The Strategist
259, 295, 529, 592, 925, 952-The Problem Solver
268, 286, 628, 682, 826, 862-The Rescuer
269, 296, 629, 692, 926, 962-The Good Samaritan
278, 287, 728, 782, 827, 872-The Free Spirit
279, 297, 729, 792, 927, 972-The Peacemaker
358, 385, 538, 583, 835, 853-The Solution Master
359, 395, 539, 593, 935, 953-The Thinker
368, 386, 638, 683, 836, 863-The Justice Fighter
369, 396, 639, 693, 936, 963-The Mediator
378, 387, 738, 783, 837, 873-The Mover Shaker
379, 397, 739, 793, 937, 973-The Ambassador
458, 485, 548, 584, 845, 854-The Scholar
459, 495, 549, 594, 945, 954-The Contemplative
468, 486, 648, 684, 846, 864-The Truth Teller
469, 496, 649, 694, 946, 964-The Seeker
478, 487, 748, 784, 847, 874-The Messenger
479, 497, 749, 794, 947, 974-The Gentle Spirit

Do any of these descriptions resonate with you better? Surely one would. And last but not least, there is another important component of what influences your Enneagram type that go beyond the personality types, the wings, and even the Tritypes. Let's now look at the subtypes which are also found through the works of Dr. Claudio Naranjo, and are further explored by Katherine Chernick Fauvre. That will be covered in the next chapter, and you will also learn about how other areas of your natal chart go hand in hand with the subtypes of the Enneagram.

The Instinctual Types and Subtypes

IF YOU THOUGHT we were one with the Enneagram, you were wrong because just how it is with astrology, there are so many parts to the Enneagram that must be covered in this book since it is quite relevant. However, we are going to keep it as basic as possible so there is not any type of information overload.

As far as the Enneagram goes, we have already covered the personality types, the arrows, the wings, the centers, the Tritypes, and now it is time to talk about the Instinctual Subtypes.

There are several terms that are associated with the Instinctual Subtypes, and this term along with Instinctual Types, is used by Katherine Chernick Fauvre. However, other terms to describe this part of the Enneagram are "rives instincts, and subtypes. And, Katherine Chernick Fauvre has stated that Oscar Ichazo used the terms "drives" and instincts for the centers as the instincts. Naranjo added to Ichazo's work by identifying the instinctual "subtypes' for this area of the Enneagram back in his teachings.

Fauvre also stated that Dr. Claudio Naranjo in 1969 along with others was trained with Oscar Ichazo in Arica, Chile in the Enneagram. From 1971-1973 Dr. Claudio Naranjo had established the Seekers After Truth or SAT groups in Berkeley, California where he taught the Enneagram as well as the Subtypes in his own lectures.

And, in 1996, Dr. Claudio Naranjo which was more than 20 years later taught the Enneagram for the first time in its entirety and the Instinctual Subtypes on a deeper level through his perspective in Boulder, Colorado.

Oscar Ichazo has taught that the drives, according to Katherine Chernick Fauvre, as *three fundamental reactions of our organism in order to sustain life*. In other words, he taught that instincts are based on how our basic psychological level functions in order to survive.

Dr. Claudio Naranjo added to Oscar on instincts. As Katherine Chernick Fauvre has stated in her work, Dr. Claudio Naranjo found that the instinctual type is *one of three sub-personalities that is the 'auxiliary passion'*. On the outside, anyone can appear as if they have a gift or a talent that they want to show off, but deep down, there is a level of unhappiness.

Dr. Claudio Naranjo also has taught that there is a drive as well as the origin of each subtype. There is the self-preservation subtype which is associated with the protection of the self which arises in the gut area, there is the social subtype that indicates the need to find a place in the world as well as to be appreciated which arises in the tongue. And, there is the sexual subtype, which is also referred to as the intimate or one on one subtype which is self-explanatory, which arises from the genital area.

That means there are three Instinctual Subtypes that everyone has which are Self-Preserving, Social, and Sexual. And, everyone has a dominant subtype. The dominant subtype is the instinct that is the most present and influential in your personality.

Let's now take a look at each of the Instinctual Subtypes as well as how areas in the natal chart can determine which ones anyone would have.

Self-Preservation

The self-preserving Instinctual Subtype or SP is what focuses on ways to preserve the body's well-being and physical survival and safety. That can go for physical comfort as well, and the need for any type of material which includes food, shelter, clothing, conservation, protection, and warmth. The fears that are associated with SP are illness, loss, endangerment, poverty, suspense, and being annihilated. The matching element for SP would be earth. The SP subtype is what causes us to look within and worry about our own needs. Let's now take a quick look at the 9 SP subtypes:

SP 1 - The key subtype would be worry, and the ongoing desire to keep things under control. Those with the 1 SP tend to find reasons to expect any type of risk as well as complications and problems. They have a very intense inner critic and are extremely harsh on themselves because they expect too much of themselves. They do everything they can to be prepared and make sure they are prepared for anything that involves making sure all bases are covered to the smallest detail. They don't like to express anger but they do feel deep frustration when they are triggered. Those that have a 6th house stellium or a lot of planets in Virgo regardless of where they are may have a 1 SP.

SP 2 - Those who have the 2 SP focus on tending to the needs of the one that can tend to their needs because they bring that out in others. They want to be taken care of but at the same time, do not want to depend on others either. They seek a secure relationship where they will take care of another to be taken care of. They are the iron fist in the velvet glove. They easily feel rejected and when they do, they become withdrawn. They are also seen as feeling entitled. Those who have a lot of either Leo or Pisces energy, such as a 12th house stellium, a 5th house stellium, or a stellium in Pisces or Leo (especially if Leo happens to be on the 4th, 8th, or 12th house cusp) regardless of house placements may likely be a 2 SP.

SP 3 - This particular Instinctual Subtype is contradictory. Those who are SP 3 may not overtly show off their accomplishments and strengths too much and don't like to appear that they are all about images. Yet at the same time, they want to be acknowledged for their hard work. They are extremely productive and efficient. Security is very important to them, and want to be as self-sufficient as much as possible. However, this can cause them to become workaholics as well. Those who have a Virgo stellium, or planets in the 6th house can very likely be a 3 SP.

SP 4 - This Instinctual Subtype is also contradictory because type 4 is associated with being emotional and dramatic. However, those who are 4 SP have found a way to cope with pain and have internalized it. They appear stoic but at the same time, they are sensitive. They like to share their feelings with others however at the same time they are empathetic and are supportive towards others who suffer. Those who have a lot of Aquarian energy in their charts or who have a stellium in the 11th house may be a 4 SP. They care for the welfare of others but disconnect from their own feelings and pain.

SP 5 - Those who are an SP 5 are extremely protective of their personal space, which they see as their castle, and are very private. They will make their boundaries known and set limits. They are quite content with being alone and having a few good friends but for the most part, are introverted and prefer to live more of a solitary life. They keep their guard up high due to the fact that they value their privacy. Those who have planets in Scorpio or a full 8th house (and full water houses in general) are likely to have this Instinctual Subtype.

SP 6 - Those who are an SP 6 want to feel safe and feel the need to build relationships with others in order to have that sense of security. They are very warm and kind to those who they are close to and use friendliness with new people to check out if people can be trusted. They don't like to show anger but will do so if they feel threatened. Those who have this Instinctual Subtype have a lot of Libra energy in their charts meaning they have plenty of planets in Libra or have a stellium in the 7th house.

SP 7 - Those who have this SP subtype create a network of like-minded people as their 'family' to insure security and enjoyment. They do want the best for everyone in their circle that is involved, but at the same time, they are wanting to find the best things in life due to the fact that they have strong pleasure-seeking tendencies. They want to seek enjoyment and have fun but will defend their own. They seek freedom and will even defend their choices in for that to happen even if those choices are considered to be poor choices. Those who have this Instinctual Subtype likely have either a lot of Gemini or Sagittarian energy or stelliums in the 9th or 3rd houses.

SP 8 - Those who have this SP subtype are quite powerful, bold, productive, and are very direct. They are also quite confident no matter how challenging the situation is. They are seen as pillars of strength and have been able to survive tough situations. They protect their own. However, when they feel betrayed, and feel their needs have not been met, they can become extremely irritated and will make it clear that they will not stand for not getting what they need and feel entitled to. They will take a direct approach to get it and will not allow anything or anyone to get into the way. Those who have this Instinctual Subtype would likely have a lot of planets in Aries or has a stellium in the 1st house.

SP 9 - Those who have this Instinctual Subtype is known for being kind. They seek harmony and ease. They can easily give in to the physical pleasures such as sleeping, eating, and even reading. This can be seen as an escape for comfort, and those who have this SP will appear to be upset and stubborn if anything or anyone to get into the way of their comfort. This Instinctual Subtype is also indicated by plenty of planets in Taurus or a stellium in the 2nd house, especially if Venus is present.

Is your self-preservation subtype dominant? Let's now take a look at the Social Instinctive Subtype.

Social Instinctive Subtype

The Social Instinctive Subtype or as it is referred to as SO is defined by how you get along with others, and form relationships. Whereas the SP represents your survival instincts by having your own needs met, the SO represents your social instincts. It indicates how you form bonds, how you create relationships, how you get along in groups and communities. This instinct represents and focuses on how the energy is used by working towards a purpose that is shared, or for the well-being of all around you.

The desires that are shown through this subtype are recognition, popularity, status, and honor. The deepest fears that are indicated by the SO are being isolated, inferior, the outcast, ranking low, being lonely, and failure. It shows how you relate to others, or how you do not. The element this subtype matches is air.

Let's now take a quick look at the characteristics of the 9 SO subtypes.

SO1 - Those who have this Instinctual Subtype only want to bring attention to what is right and appropriate. They have high standards, are quite righteous, and will not accept anything that is out of balance and that is unfair. They are very rigid and are quite non-adaptable. Those who have this as their dominant SO will likely have the Virgo cusp on the 3rd, 7th, or 11th houses, as well as a stellium. They most likely would have this placement in the 7th house, but any of the air houses could be an indicator.

SO2 - Those who have this Instinctual Subtype is quite ambitious, and take on the leadership role as they stand out from the crowd. They have great aspirations, a strong drive, and are devoted to building their communities. They are highly influential, and for those who have this dominant subtype would easily be mistaken for being a type 3 or a type 8. Those who have this subtype as their dominant one would likely have fire signs (Aries, Leo, Sagittarius) on the cusp of their air houses, as well as a stellium in it. Especially the 11th house.

SO3 - Those who are an SO 3 are highly concerned about prestige, and their achievements, and having recognition and accolades is highly important to them. They are extremely competitive, and always want to be in the spotlight due to having success. They will cover up any type of imperfection as long as their finished product or creation is highly marketable. Those who have this as their dominant subtype would either have Leo or Capricorn on the cusp of any of their air houses and a stellium in it.

SO4 - Those who have this as their subtype are extremely sensitive emotionally, and they are quite connected to how they have suffered and how they do suffer. In fact, they find comfort in how they suffer and make it known to others so they can get the support they crave. They really want to be understood, and often are full of self-doubt. They compare themselves to others and blame themselves for things that go wrong. They also struggle with shame and envy. Those who have this subtype as their dominant one would likely have Scorpio or Pisces on any of their air house cusps in addition to a stellium.

SO5 - Those who have this subtype are quite inquisitive that they are searching for any deep meaning in a situation, and they are looking to connect with groups so they can not only share their ideas and wisdom but where they can learn from others and expand their knowledge base. Even though they are eager to share their ideas, wisdom, and knowledge, they do not want to share their own personal space. In fact, they are more likely to be involved in secret societies so they expand their wisdom but are not easily found by just anyone. Those who have Aquarius on the cusp of any of their air houses in addition to a stellium may have this subtype as their dominant one.

Another possible placement would be Scorpio on their 3rd house cusp or Pluto or Mars in their 3rd house (or possibly 9th) which would explain their desire to keep learning but to remain private.

SO6 - Those who have this subtype are often thought of as being a type 1 because they follow the rules. However, they are also the type to stick up for the underdog and are dutiful, rational, and make it known that following the rules is very important. Those who have this as their dominant subtype may have Libra on their 7th house cusp, but would more likely to have a stellium in their 6th house. And even though the 6th house is not an air house, those who have a strong Virgo influence that is seen in other areas of the chart may display the SO 6 as their dominant subtype.

SO7 - Those that have the SO7 are thought to have the type 2. Those who have this subtype are generous and want to be there for others. They will sacrifice themselves to make sure everyone else benefits in exchange for recognition. However, they also can be extremely judgemental if they feel they haven't given enough or if others don't show appreciation for what they have done. Those who have this subtype as their dominant one likely have Cancer on the cusp of one of their air houses and a stellium in Cancer as well.

SO8 - Those who have this subtype are focused on friends and foes. If a friend, they use their influence to help others and to support them instead of them wanting to be in control like the typical SP type 8. They are also loyal and protective of those who they are close to and will keep them away from anything that could potentially be harmful.

Just like the typical type 8, they don't want to expose their vulnerabilities but are willing to do so to those who they trust and will listen to constructive criticism in order to better themselves. Those who have this subtype as the dominant one are likely to have either Mars in Libra in any of the houses, or may have Scorpio on any of the air house cusp.

Those who have Scorpio on the air houses may be shown as the SO 4 or 5 in the case of it being on the 3rd house cusp. However, that also depends on the rest of the placements in the natal chart.

SO9 - Those who have this subtype participate in groups and will even take on the role as the mediator, and will not hesitate to put on a happy facade and hide their own issues in order to keep everyone else happy. In fact, in some cases, they may even be the facilitator in groups to make sure everyone else's needs are being met. They will not acknowledge their pain and will hide their stress, and can fall into workaholism as a result.

Those who have this as their dominant subtype will likely have Venus in any of their air houses or may have Libra as the cusp of any of their air houses. There are some parallels between this subtype and SO6.

Is your SO type dominant? Now, let's take a look at the last group of Instinctual Subtypes which is the One to One or Sexual Subtype.

The One to One or Sexual Subtype

This Instinctual Subtype is the last group of subtypes, and it represents how you project yourself in one on one relationships, how you connect with others intimately, and it is the One to One or Sexual Subtype which is also referred to as SX. This represents sex appeal, encounters, intrigue, glamor, union, eye contact, and anything that is intimate.

The desires that this subtype represents is finding the other half to become whole, closeness, and affinity. The biggest fears that this subtype represents are being disconnected, being unworthy, letting go, being incomplete, loss of appeal, and being invalidated. This subtype matches 2 elements which would be water and fire. Let's take a look at the 9 SX subtypes now and you will find one that resonates with you the most.

SX1 - Those who have SX1 as their subtype would express jealousy, and would expect others to do anything that they feel is right. They feel entitled to insist that others do things that they would only do. In fact, those who have this subtype may appear to have unhealthy traits of the type 8. And those who have this subtype would likely have Mars or Pluto in the 4th or 8th houses or would have Scorpio on either of those houses.

SX2 - Those who have this subtype is known to be seductive, and know how to build strong and intense relationships. And once they trust someone they know how to make their needs known. They can be quite passionate and strong-willed, and even aggressive. They are extremely devoted but have high expectations and will not accept no for an answer. Those who have this placement may have Venus or Uranus in the 8th house.

SX3 - Those who have this subtype are enthusiastic and are full of charisma, and the way that they are competitive is by supporting their desired other. That is because they hold the belief that if others are successful around them, then that makes them successful. They will compete for the love and attention of those who they care for the most, and will do anything they can to make themselves attractive to their mate which means even suppressing their feelings. Those who have this subtype are likely to have a strong Venus in the 8th house, or Taurus or Libra on the cusp with a stellium.

SX4 - Those who have this subtype appear to have no shame unlike the social type 4. They are demanding that others appreciate them and that they become controlling to the point that they would end up becoming rejected which would make them angry and frustrated. They are comfortable making it known how angry they are. However, they hide very well how upset and confused they really are. Those who have this placement may have Neptune in the 8th house or Pisces on the cusp with a stellium which would likely include Mars.

SX5 - Those who have this subtype seek confidence and trust. They will focus on a passionate life in private. In fact, they feel a strong connection with those who they are truly passionate about and will be very open. They do end up depending on the other to make them feel alive and full of vitality. Those who have this subtype would likely have Sagittarius on the 8th house cusp or Jupiter in the 8th house.

SX6 - Those who have this subtype are known to be quite provocative, rebellious, bold, assertive, and instead of running away from anything that appears to be intimidating like a typical 6 - they would run towards it and challenge it. In fact, those who have SX6 would be thought of as those who have a type 8 personality.

The placements that you would see in a chart that can be an indicator of someone who has this subtype would either be Uranus in the 5th house or Leo on the 8th house cusp with Mars or even Uranus in the 6th house.

SX7 - Those who have this subtype are the types who want to see the good in everyone and have rose-colored glasses on, and are quite charming. They are fascinated easily and are the dreamer, and extremely idealistic. They are striving to see the world being brighter than it is, and will easily want to see reality embellished.

They will, however, grow bored in relationships that they find boring. Those who have Neptune in the 5th house may end up having this subtype. Even though the 7th house is an air house or a social house, Neptune in the 7th can be an indicator as well.

SX8 - Those who have this subtype are very protective of intimates. They are quite possessive and are defiant. The SX8 has a strong need for intensity, and want to be powerful. In fact, they have a strong urge to create change and will not have a problem with disrupting the lives of others in order to bring it. They may have this desire to bring out change for a positive reason but they also do it from a place of wanting to be in control. Those who have this subtype may have Pluto or Uranus in either the 4th, 5th, or 8th house.

SX9 - Those who have this subtype are not comfortable with being on their own and only find security being in relationship with others. As long as they have partners, they are happy and secure. They will even sacrifice their own needs and wants if someone else they are partnered with wants something completely different. They will agree to do it and will not pay attention to their own needs. Those who have Libra on the 5th or 8th house cusps along with a stellium may end up having this subtype, or Venus. Possibly the on the 12th house cusp as well.

However, with Venus in the 12th, that can signify secret relationships and affairs which may also happen with an SX9 if they are finding security in that instead of the relationship that they may be in. That all depends on the other aspects of the personality and the natal chart.

That concludes the section on the Instinctual Subtypes. Have you determined what your dominant subtype happens to be?

Conclusion

WHEN IT COMES to learning about who we are, and why our personalities are the way they are, and how we can make ourselves better, there are so many fascinating tools that will teach us what we need to know about ourselves. These tools teach us what we value, and why we like the things we do, and why we dislike the things we do. These tools give us a good understanding of why we react to stimuli in the environment the way we do, and how we find comfort, and why we are prone to developing certain habits as well.

That is why astrology has been a fantastic tool for thousands of years in order to not only teach us about the energies we are going to be encountering through transits - but it is a tool that teaches us who we are and why have our likes, dislikes, and helps us understand our personalities.

And, when you combine astrology with the Enneagram system which is another fantastic tool, you even get a much better understanding of your personality and why you are the way you are. Not only do you have a tool that will help you be on a path to self-acceptance, but you have these tools that will help you better yourself, become more aware of yourself, and have a better understanding of other people.

Combining astrology and the Enneagram system is an extremely powerful way to understand yourself and to understand others to the core.

References

1. *The Only Astrology Book You'll Ever Need*, Joanna Martine Woolfolk, 2012.
2. Katherine Chernick Fauvre, Originator of Enneagram Tritype® and Instinctual Stacking, IEA Accredited, Triple Certified Enneagram Trainer and Coach, https://www.katherinefauvre.com/
3. David W. Fauvre, MA, founder of Enneagram Explorations https://enneagram.net

About the Author

MIRIAM SLOZBERG IS a Canadian mother, certified astrologer, freelance writer, and a content creator. She has always had a strong interest in metaphysical and spiritual studies. She has learned a lot about herself through her own personal hardships and wants to share her wisdom with others who are struggling. She also has a strong sarcastic side that she is quite proud of having. She is proud to be unique and is a typical Enneagram type 4 with a strong 5 wing, with a Leo Sun, Taurus Moon, and Sagittarius Rising.

Printed in the United States
By Bookmasters